Eric Barger is one of the most gifted presenters of biblical truth I have been privileged to have minister in my church. Eric excels in his research, documentation, and Bible content, and he ministers with the anointing of the Holy Spirit, bringing conviction to our hearts in each of his studies. Eric Barger has been called to be a watchman who has taken his calling seriously and without regard for political correctness. PTL!!!

Dr. Freddie Young
Pastor, Grand Strand Baptist Church, Myrtle Beach, SC

Recognized for many years as one of America's premier apologetics ministers, Eric Barger is well known for his sound theological treatise of Scripture. His book, *Disarming the Powers of Darkness*, however, exceeded even my high expectations. Well written, thoroughly researched, biblically accurate, and powerful both in insights and in practical applications, *Disarming the Powers of Darkness* is a must-read for every believer because *we wrestle not against flesh and blood.*

Robert B. Fort
Chairman & CEO, United Evangelical Churches

Eric Barger and David Benoit have done a masterful job providing biblical insight that will help believers understand the spiritual battle and how we can effectively operate in it. *Disarming the Powers of Darkness* is a much-needed "must-read" resource for those who desire to navigate through the waters of spiritual warfare.

Brandon Holthaus
Pastor, Rock Harbor Church, Bakersfield, CA

Eric Barger's vast knowledge of Scripture and his ability to communicate it with passion inspires me and challenges me to dig deeper in my own research. His love for our Lord Jesus, his eternal perspective, and his God-given drive to defend the faith are just a few of Eric's strengths. From apologetics to the importance of understanding spiritual warfare, his ministry is effective and vital to the equipping of the body of Christ in America.

David Fiorazo
Author and Radio Host, Green Bay, WI

I so appreciated the ministry of Eric Barger in providing scripturally sound, cutting-edge resources for the church. We have had the privilege of having Eric with us annually for the past ten years. His sound research and effective presentations have helped equip our people with spiritual discernment for many of the deceptions in our day – even within Christian churches – as well as given solid answers for some of the tough questions they encounter in their day-to-day lives. All Christians and Christian churches will benefit by utilizing the materials Eric has produced, particularly *Disarming the Powers of Darkness.*

Rick Long
Senior Pastor, Atonement Free Lutheran Church, Arlington, WA

Scan the QR Code to watch Eric's personal introduction to this book.

DISARMING THE POWERS OF DARKNESS

Manuscript edited and updated by Eric Barger, 2016

DISARMING THE **POWERS** OF **DARKNESS**

FEARLESS CONQUERORS IN SPIRITUAL WARFARE

Eric Barger
with David Benoit

Visit Eric's website: www.ericbarger.com

Disarming the Powers of Darkness – Eric Barger

For more information write: Eric Barger at Take A Stand! Ministries, PO Box 279, Spanaway, WA 98387.

Copyright © 2016

First edition published 2002

Bible version: King James Version

Cover Design: Natalia Hawthorne, BookCoverLabs.com

eBook Icon: Icon design/Shutterstock

Editors: Sheila Wilkinson and Ruth Zetek

Printed in the United States of America

Aneko Press – *Our Readers Matter*™

www.anekopress.com

Aneko Press, Life Sentence Publishing, and our logos are trademarks of

Life Sentence Publishing, Inc.
203 E. Birch Street
P.O. Box 652
Abbotsford, WI 54405

RELIGION / Christian Life / Spiritual Warfare

Paperback ISBN: 978-1-62245-346-7

eBook ISBN: 978-1-62245-347-4

10 9 8 7 6 5 4 3 2 1

Available where books are sold

Share this book on Facebook:

Contents

First and foremost, we thank the Lord by His Holy Spirit for directing our steps during the formulation of this book.

From Eric: Thanks to my wife, Melanie, who's been with me every step of the way. I couldn't ask for a better life and ministry partner.

I want to acknowledge Wayne and Louise Ivey and David and Pam McCune for their friendship and help in making this book a reality.

Special thanks also to Dee Hilt, Steve Malmquist, and Sherri Cupples for their editing and advice.

From David: Thanks to my wife, Debbie, and my family for their insight and love.

I would like to give a special thanks to Dr. Elmer and Ruth Towns. They have been a wonderful encouragement and help to both me and my wife, Debbie. Dr. and Mrs. Towns have been shot at and even wounded in this spiritual battle, yet they have refused to surrender.

Foreword

The battlefield is real and the Enemy is determined. With these two thoughts in mind, as Christians, we need to take heed of 1 Peter 5:8-10.

Be sober, be vigilant; because your adversary the devil, as a roaring lion, walketh about, seeking whom he may devour: Whom resist stedfast in the faith, knowing that the same afflictions are accomplished in your brethren that are in the world. But the God of all grace, who hath called us unto his eternal glory by Christ Jesus, after that ye have suffered a while, make you perfect, stablish, strengthen, settle you.

We learn four things from this passage:

1. The Enemy is real.

2. We win by staying steadfast.

3. We are not in the battle alone.

4. After the pain, there will be gain.

Many Christians today suffer from battle fatigue, and with

good reason. The front line of this spiritual battle is everywhere. Whether at home, work, school, or even church, we are under heavy fire and the casualties are enormous. What Christians need to understand is that there is no Geneva Convention designed to protect those captured in the battle. This Enemy will show no mercy to those who surrender to him.

As the pastor of Thomas Road Baptist Church for over forty-six years, I have seen the wounded firsthand. Our staff has had to wrap abused, neglected, and battered women in loving and caring arms. We have counseled the POWs of this spiritual war. Their tormenters were drugs, alcohol, pornography, illicit sex, and guilt, which on many occasions would drive these victims to the verge of self-destruction. Thankfully, we have had the balm of Gilead to apply to those wounded and bruised in this raging battle. The bad news is that the casualties may be great, but the good news is that we are within shouting distance of the Great Physician. We may lose some battles, but praise be to God, we will win the war.

> *Who shall separate us from the love of Christ? shall
> tribulation, or distress, or persecution, or famine,
> or nakedness, or peril, or sword? As it is written,
> For thy sake we are killed all the day long; we are
> accounted as sheep for the slaughter. Nay, in all
> these things we are more than conquerors through
> him that loved us.* – Romans 8:35-37

As the chancellor of Liberty University for thirty years, my goal has always been to turn out champions – young people who will fight the good fight and keep the faith. Mediocrity is never found in the vocabulary of a true champion. A good soldier will stay focused and will not get sidetracked.

> *Thou therefore endure hardness, as a good soldier
> of Jesus Christ. No man that warreth entangleth*

himself with the affairs of this life; that he may please him who hath chosen him to be a soldier. And if a man also strive for masteries, yet is he not crowned, except he strive lawfully. – 2 Timothy 2:3-5

I am afraid that most Christian soldiers today are dressed for the ballroom, not the battlefield. We know that God will one day issue formal attire followed by an awards banquet we'll never forget, but for now, it is battle attire we must wear. May the pages of this book, *Disarming the Powers of Darkness*, be a source of encouragement and strength for every soldier who strives to be all that he or she can be for God.

Dr. Jerry Falwell
Pastor, Thomas Road Baptist Church
Founder, Liberty University
Lynchburg, VA

Introduction

The Call to War

For we wrestle not against flesh and blood, but against principalities, against powers, against the rulers of the darkness of this world, against spiritual wickedness in high places. – Ephesians 6:12

If thou forbear to deliver them that are drawn unto death, and those that are ready to be slain; If thou sayest, Behold, we knew it not; doth not he that pondereth the heart consider it? and he that keepeth thy soul, doth not he know it? and shall not he render to every man according to his works?
– Proverbs 24:11-12

*D*isarming the Powers of Darkness is about personal victory for you and your home in spiritual warfare. As the second Scripture passage above proclaims, our utmost responsibility as Christians is to rescue those being led away to death. We cannot shrink from it. It is because of this that we feel so passionately about this issue. Our goal is to teach and live biblical truths, expose Satan's ploys, and lift up Jesus Christ as the only hope. And we hope that you will be inspired by this book and will strive to do likewise. However, we've already used a phrase that confuses or even frightens many today – *spiritual warfare*. But fear not, you can have victory and you can win in the spiritual war!

In the 1980s and '90s, we heard lots of discussion about spiritual warfare. Just about everywhere you looked within Christendom, someone was talking about some form of warfare. It became a buzzword. In the process, excesses surfaced, demonism and deliverance became frightening for some, and true victory in Christ became obscured and seemed unattainable for many. There truly is no shortage of differing views on this controversial issue.

Some evangelicals exhibit confusion on the issue by ignoring some of the more intense aspects of spiritual warfare such as demon possession. On the other hand, some believers tend to see a demon behind every door and under every rock, when in fact, many of the sicknesses and sins plaguing mankind are simply a continuation of original sin (Genesis 3). Furthermore, some of those caught in the trap of spiritual liberalism completely disavow the very existence of the Devil – let alone any intrusion into the lives of humans by his demonic forces – and are thus easy targets for his deceptions. So what is the truth and where is the balance?

The "90-10" Approach

While we firmly believe in Satan's work being a reality in the world, and fully concur that demons exist and often need to be cast out of the possessed, this is not the focus of this book. Many terrific resources are available today that deal with deliverance and related topics. While we certainly won't leave issues pertaining to the demonic untouched, our desire is to instill the need for every Christian to fight and win the battle for personal victory on an everyday scale. When called to battle, far too many saints seem ill prepared to deal effectively with the demonic because they are not victorious as a habit. Thus, we have given this section the title: "The '90-10' Approach." Dealing directly with the demonic is perhaps 10 percent of spiritual warfare, while living in a state of victory and personal freedom makes up the other 90 percent. If we do this, we'll be ready, willing, and able – in season and out – when Satan and his minions rear their ugly heads for a personal confrontation.

Spiritual warfare, understanding it and waging it, is paramount to our spiritual effectiveness and survival until we're at home in heaven. Every day is the time to be alert and aware of the Enemy's plans, actions, and desires. Yet with so many different viewpoints, where do we begin? Is there a balance? Yes! To capitalize on knowing God's Word and serving Him daily is, of course, our first priority. Concurrently, the defeat of mankind's three enemies – the world, the flesh, and the Devil – must be a priority too.

The apostle Peter admonishes us:

> *Be sober, be vigilant; because your adversary the devil, as a roaring lion, walketh about, seeking whom he may devour: Whom resist stedfast in the faith, knowing that the same afflictions are accomplished in your brethren that are in the world.*
> – 1 Peter 5:8-9

Satan is out to trick, trap, and destroy whomever he can, and he and his forces are at work all over the earth doing just that. The antidote for this is twofold. First, it is found in a flourishing, vibrant relationship with Jesus Christ. He is King of Kings and conquering Lord. We must be conscious that our victory is not based on our efforts and intentions but is only available as we abide in Him. Second, it is found in obedience to studying, understanding, and implementing what the Lord imparted to us in His Word. So with that in mind, here is the reason we think this book is important, regardless of whether you are a single adult, grandparent, teenager, or parent. There is a level of victory – spiritual power – that many in modern Christianity are missing.

We believe one important reason for this widespread anemic condition is that Satan's attacks often go unnoticed in our lives and homes. We have become anesthetized to the Devil's workings. Because of this, the subtle influences that seep through the cracks in our humanity soon root themselves as fixtures in our lives.

Many Christians shout "Amen!" when there is mention of the defeat of Satan, his workers, and his power. However, when we talk about personal responsibility and taking action in spiritual warfare, the chorus of "amens" subsides into a murmur of "oh, my" and "who, me?" Understanding the very real threat the Enemy presents to us daily is a matter of paramount importance to our families. However, most modern-day Christians do not care to hear this because it requires two key things: time, which we claim we don't have enough of; and action, which we simply don't want to take. We have learned that when we stand up to preach about this in seminars nationwide, even the most astute churchgoers often find their feathers ruffled. The general reaction is this:

> "My home? Spiritual warfare in my home? Surely, you are kidding. Do you think I'm living in sin or something? Are you suggesting that I change the way I live or the things that entertain me and my kids? No way! I'm a good Christian. You are a radical. Just keep your nose out of my business."

Though it's not often verbalized to us, experience tells us that this is, in fact, the way many folks react when confronted with the need to take action or make a change.

Yes, this book may agitate some who read it. We know that. But our hope is that by exposing the issues, discussing biblical precepts, and offering our insights and suggestions, you will benefit, and the body of Christ will be strengthened.

What You Don't Know Will Hurt You

For many years, we have written and taught about spiritual warfare and its effect on the home and family. We've seen many folks choose to be winners in this warfare, and we praise the Lord for this and are grateful that somehow we played a part in strengthening His church. Sadly, we've also watched many try to ignore the need to engage in the spiritual battle and subsequently pay the consequences. During those years of ministry in this area, we think we've found a key.

The late, prolific apologist Dr. Walter Martin once quoted his mentor, Donald Grey Barnhouse, as saying, "You've got to get the hay down out of the loft where the cows can get at it." We concur. Much of what we've read on spiritual warfare has seemed unattainable to the average member of Christ's church, being either out of reach or ominous, spooky, and threatening. Our goal is to take the wraps off spiritual warfare and expose some of the deceptions that affect many today. We're going to make it as simple and understandable as possible so everyone reading can grasp and then implement God's Word on warfare. We want to caution you that often any commitment made to spiritual victory won't be pretty, and it won't be easy, but it will be worth it. Our prayer for the reader is that you and your household may go on to be the victors in Christ Jesus that God has called you to be!

Go with us now as we take a no-nonsense look at some

important areas of Christian living that many people would just rather not deal with. Along the way through these pages, if God speaks to your heart about adjustments in attitudes or behavior, we encourage you to allow the Holy Spirit room to operate. He'll never direct a change arbitrarily, but always because He's a Father who loves you and wants you to walk in the victory He's provided through His Son at the cross. The need for victorious spiritual warriors continues to increase, and the battle is surely intensifying as we move on through these prophetic last days. We pray that you'll do more than just "amen" us and that you'll examine your life and your home with fresh, biblical understanding. If you do, we believe that you and your family will see a very real and powerful difference for eternity's sake.

One last thing: Our victory over darkness isn't just for our benefit. It's also for the good of others and for the furthering of the kingdom of God. If we enter into battle merely motivated by "self," then we've fallen into the trap of the world today. If we view the steps we take in spiritual warfare as acts of obedience to the Lord, we'll then be in a position to watch God do some great and awesome things in our own lives.

– Eric Barger & David Benoit, June 2002

Chapter 1

You ARE in a WAR

For though we walk in the flesh, we do not war after the flesh. – 2 Corinthians 10:3

Every Christian's life is a warfare with Satan, and his principalities and powers, with the world, the men and lusts of it, and with the corruptions of their own hearts; and much more is the life of a minister of the Gospel, who is called forth to meet the adversary in the gate; to stand in the hottest place of the battle, and sustain the whole fire and artillery of the enemy; to fight the good fight of faith, endure hardness as a good soldier of Christ, and with the weapons he is furnished with to war a good warfare: which is not done "after the flesh"; in such a manner as the men of the world wage war with one another; or upon carnal principles; or with carnal selfish views; or in a weak way and manner; but in a spiritual way, with all simplicity and disinterested views, with great courage and intrepidity of mind.
– John Gill, Pastor, Strict Baptist Church, 1720-1771

Since the first confrontation with Lucifer in the garden of Eden, mankind has been engaged in a spiritual struggle.

Whether you want to acknowledge it or not, we are all in a spiritual war. The hard reality is that if you are breathing, you are in this war and will be in it until you take your last breath here on earth. While this statement may be a revelation to some, it may well be dismissed by others; but nonetheless, it is true.

Many Christians seem to believe that somehow they are immune to this fact. We know that every born-again believer has been positionally delivered from the kingdom of darkness, as Colossians 1 declares. But this deliverance from being members of Satan's kingdom does not exclude us from his attacks. In fact, they are an inevitability we can count on. Your position as a believer does not change Satan's plan for your life. His desire is to continue to steal, kill, and destroy. Thankfully, however, in the same verse where we learn this, Jesus tells us of His own plan, which is to give us life and life more abundantly (John 10:10). That is the difference. Before we became Christians, we had no defense and probably little or no understanding of the Evil One. Now, covered in Jesus' righteousness, we can be victorious over the ruler of darkness and his forces. Regardless, though, every reader seeing these words is indeed in a war, as is every other person living on the planet. The real questions are: whose side are you fighting on, and which kingdom are you a part of?

Many saints of God unrealistically desire to be permanently immune from knowing about, being subject to, or participating in spiritual warfare. As pleasant as this may sound, it's not going to happen until we get to heaven. The fact is, as long as we're here, we are going to be in the arena of spiritual warfare.

However, if our hearts and lives are right before God, warfare may often be likened to sitting inside an armored tank. An adversary outside may be shooting a small-caliber weapon at it, and those inside the tank may indeed be aware of the assault, feeling the concussion of the bullets as they strike. However, regardless of the knowledge or awareness of the attack, those inside the tank are protected from the potentially deadly – yet inferior – assault taking place. Yes, a war is going on, but they will not be harmed in the battle. In fact, the weapons at their disposal from inside the protective covering are far more powerful than anything the enemy has to offer. Just one shot from the tank's cannon and the enemy is toast. Praise God!

The Biblical Proof of the Spiritual War

To the skeptic, it is important for you to understand that we are Bible believers who believe in the inerrancy and sufficiency of Scripture from Genesis through Revelation. We believe that if a person makes claims of being a Christian, then he or she should understand the complete and utter reliance that Christians should have on the Word of God. That being the case, please carefully examine the following Scriptures, which clearly announce that there is an ongoing spiritual conflict between the kingdom of darkness and the army of God.

> *For we wrestle not against flesh and blood, but against principalities, against powers, against the rulers of the darkness of this world, against spiritual wickedness in high places.* – Ephesians 6:12

Our warfare is not waged against humans, but against the echelons of evil in the spirit realm.

> *Submit yourselves therefore to God. Resist the devil, and he will flee from you.* James 4:7

Walking under the lordship and command of God while making a stand against the adversary guarantees ultimate freedom.

> *Beloved, when I gave all diligence to write unto you of the common salvation, it was needful for me to write unto you, and exhort you that ye should*

*earnestly contend for the faith which was once deliv-
ered unto the saints.* – Jude 3

If there were not a war and an Enemy attempting to steal and
pervert our faith, then why would God's Word instruct us
about the need to contend for it? While we must be ready to
give every man answers for why we believe (1 Peter 3:15), the
evidence from Scripture here indicates that we are to be mindful of the Enemy's accusations against the truth.

> *Be sober, be vigilant; because your adversary the
> devil, as a roaring lion, walketh about, seeking
> whom he may devour: Whom resist stedfast in the
> faith, knowing that the same afflictions are accom-
> plished in your brethren that are in the world.*
> – 1 Peter 5:8-9

In 1 Chronicles 12, we're told about the leaders of the tiny tribe
of Issachar who had an understanding of the times in which they
lived and knew how to respond in those times. In the passage
from Peter's first epistle, God instructs that we are to be constantly alert, ready, comprehending our Enemy and the danger
he represents, and understanding that he is seeking someone
to devour. Note that Peter says *whom he may devour*, which
indicates that he can't get everybody – only those unaware of
how to resist him. We also see here that Satan is on a worldwide mission to inflict damage on Christians. (So much for the
wishful but erroneous teaching which perpetuates the lie that
Christians are immune to spiritual attack.)

> *But I beseech you, that I may not be bold when I
> am present with that confidence, wherewith I think
> to be bold against some, which think of us as if we
> walked according to the flesh. For though we walk
> in the flesh, we do not war after the flesh: (For the
> weapons of our warfare are not carnal, but mighty*

through God to the pulling down of strong holds;)
Casting down imaginations, and every high thing
that exalteth itself against the knowledge of God,
and bringing into captivity every thought to the obe-
dience of Christ; – 2 Corinthians 10:2-5

We cannot expect to win any popularity contests for speaking up about waging spiritual warfare. Many around us attempt to deal with spiritual issues by using completely worldly means. That is what Paul is referring to here in 2 Corinthians 10:2. For example, what is the first remedy the world employs when someone exhibits signs of demon possession? Secular psychiatry, of course. If a few visits to the shrink don't fix the problem, then certainly a prescription or two will do it. All the while, the victim is probably receiving nothing more than medication to disguise the symptoms, but absolutely nothing to eliminate the cause.

That's why we can't afford to fall into the trap of *walk[ing] according to the flesh*, as have the majority of those with careers in the psychiatric health community today. Please note that, while we're certainly not opposed to doctors or medicine in general, secular psychiatry cannot cure the demon-possessed and can at best only rearrange a person's emotional and mental problems. However, Doctor Jesus can cure them completely, set them free, and make the broken soul whole.

Moving on in 2 Corinthians 10:2-5, we see other important information relative to our discussion of spiritual warfare. Verse 3 states: *For though we walk in the flesh, we do not war after the flesh.* An accurate translation of this could be: "Though we live in natural, human bodies on the earth, we do not carry out acts of warfare in the same way and with the same means that the armies of the world do." Again, the underlying point here is that Scripture clearly indicates Christians are in a war. It is interesting that the apostle Paul doesn't stop here to elaborate. He just announces: "we wage war, but not as the world does." One would think that the carnally minded Corinthians would have needed a little more instruction about this, but the Holy Spirit didn't think so. Perhaps Paul had preached on this while with them at Corinth. However, it would appear that two thousand years later many Christians seem unaware of this simple yet vital fact.

Verse 4 holds the keys to demolishing the strongholds of the Devil through the power of God, and in verse 5, the apostle Paul outlines exactly where the battlefield is and why so many end up on the losing end in spiritual warfare.

> *Casting down imaginations, and every high thing*
> *that exalteth itself against the knowledge of God,*
> *and bringing into captivity every thought to the obe-*
> *dience of Christ;* – 2 Corinthians 10:5

The battleground of spiritual warfare is the mind, and it may be that our old conceptions about warfare need to be retooled, or perhaps we simply need God's truth to fill the void of ignorance. Either way, if our thoughts run contrary to God's changeless Word by allowing antibiblical arguments, pretensions, and thoughts to dwell there, we're destined to be less than what Jesus' sacrifice ensured we could become. So if this "spiritual warfare" stuff seems foreign to you, or you've never heard about it before, or perhaps have been taught against it, we invite and encourage you to take captive every thought and make it obedient to God's Word. Change your mind and get in agreement with God. You'll be glad you did.

So once we ascertain that a war is indeed going on, what is first under attack?

Satan's First Point of Attack – The Word of God

Study to show thyself approved unto God, a work-
man that needeth not to be ashamed, rightly divid-
ing the word of truth. – 2 Timothy 2:15

One need only examine the early pages of the Bible to see that
Satan's first assault on mankind was his attack on the validity
of God's word. Inferring that God didn't really say what He
said, and that He really didn't mean it if He indeed said it, led
to the fall of mankind into original sin. It doesn't take long to
realize that the Devil hasn't changed his tactics and they are
still working some six thousand years later.

Today, theological institutions, churches, denominations,
and seminaries that not long ago preached the authentic gospel message, have tragically become shallow, empty tombs,
resorting to the social doctrines of a worthless gospel that
does little more than tickle the ears. It is not as if God didn't
give us ample warning about the current conditions of some
sectors of the church.

For men shall be lovers of their own selves, covetous,
boasters, proud, blasphemers, … Traitors, heady,
highminded, lovers of pleasures more than lovers of
God; Having a form of godliness, but denying the
power thereof: from such turn away…. Ever learn-
ing, and never able to come to the knowledge of the
truth. – 2 Timothy 3:2a, 4-5, 7

For the time will come when they will not endure
sound doctrine; but after their own lusts shall they
heap to themselves teachers, having itching ears;
And they shall turn away their ears from the truth,
and shall be turned unto fables. – 2 Timothy 4:3-4

Maintaining sound doctrine in these perilous times may indeed be our biggest battlefield. Indeed, we cannot be effective in any other area of spiritual warfare without first examining, understanding, and then firmly standing on the essentials of God's Word.

People all over the proverbial landscape claim to be Christians, yet disavow the historic central doctrines of the faith, which have been passed on to us by the apostles, the early church fathers, and the Lord Jesus Christ Himself. Though this book focuses in a different direction than simply preaching basic beliefs, we would be remiss if we did not mention that the readers will find no lasting victory in spiritual warfare unless they first ground themselves in the foundational doctrines of the faith.

Perhaps the disagreement and confusion about spiritual warfare exists among those claiming to be Christians because of the large doctrinal void in the lives of many who, by doing little more than claiming the name of Christ, are ensnared in an ongoing battle with satanic forces. The point is, find out what the Bible teaches, read it, learn it, and hang on to it. This is the key to everlasting victory over the forces of darkness around which everything revolves.

Chapter 2

The Ground Rules for Warfare

Knowing Your Enemy and Knowing Who You Are

And you hath he [Jesus] quickened, who were dead in trespasses and sins; Wherein in time past ye walked according to the course of this world, according to the prince of the power of the air, the spirit that now worketh in the children of disobedience.
– Ephesians 2:1-2

And the great dragon was cast out, that old serpent, called the Devil, and Satan, which deceiveth the whole world: he was cast out into the earth, and his angels were cast out with him. – Revelation 12:9

Scouting the Opposition

Satan. Lucifer. The Devil. The Prince of Darkness. The Evil One. Beelzebub. No matter which name we use to refer to him, he is the Enemy of mankind. He is our foe in this most important of all wars – the one for the soul. If indeed he is the

Enemy, then there must be, in fact, a conflict. If there is a conflict, then there must be a prize at stake. And if that prize is truly worth fighting for, then there should be some guidelines for winning the conflict. That is why our ministries exist and that is the reason for this book – so you and your family can be victorious in spiritual warfare.

Mad: Who, You?

As we travel each week, presenting seminars and preaching in local churches, conferences, and Christian schools, invariably we discuss the Devil and his work. Occasionally, this receives the same kind of negative reaction that our mention of spiritual warfare does. You would think that as we go to Bible-believing churches across America and mention the defeat of Satan and his powers, those in the audience would shout, "Amen!" "Hallelujah!" "Praise the Lord!"

But that is not always the case. Instead, when we mention the Devil, some people roll their eyes in disgust. Others almost yawn, seeming to question the validity of the subject. But to many folks, any mention of Satan simply makes them angry, and they may not even know why. They're not somewhat uncomfortable; they're just plain mad. Now, why is that? Perhaps our personal, individual look at spiritual warfare should begin by answering this question.

Biblical Truth vs. Political Correctness

Granted, we do our best to be straight shooters, and that, by itself, may put some folks on the defensive. You can't sit and listen to either of us teach and then get up, walk out, and say, "Well, I wonder what he really believes." There is no mistaking where we are coming from – of this, we are certain. We let you know what we stand for when we teach in person, just as we are hoping to do in these pages.

Perhaps what is disconcerting for some folks is that we teach emphatically and stand on biblical absolutes. Contrary to a culture gone mad by means of political correctness, truth isn't relative, and neither of us is interested in mincing words or softening our preaching just to be liked or accepted. Lost souls are dying out there and going into eternity without Jesus. The way we see it, every church person should evaluate what kingdom and which lord he serves. After all, the battle lines have been drawn; there are two worlds in total conflict and you cannot live successfully in both. This is why the current narcissistic and PC approach to preaching and ecclesiology that has found alarming favor across the church is a concern and actually antithetical to success in the spiritual war.

Narcissism and the "Gospel of Self"

That this is a rebellious people, lying children, children that will not hear the law of the LORD*: Which say to the seers, See not; and to the prophets, Prophesy not unto us right things, speak unto us smooth things, prophesy deceits: Get you out of the way, turn aside out of the path, cause the Holy One of Israel to cease from before us.* – Isaiah 30:9-11

We live in a world that now insists that every aspect of daily life is *or should be* about our convenience and personal feelings. Growing numbers of church attendees (particularly the postmodern age group) have wrongly accepted the creed that, like the rest of life, Sunday should be about them and what they get out of it. They want to hear what they want to hear and generally don't want to be bothered by something that may be construed in the least as "convicting." As Isaiah warned in the passage quoted above, they would rather be told lies and illusions than the hard truth. These church attendees would rather have teachers like Barger and Benoit leave all that "Devil stuff" alone and just stick to sermons on how to live a happy life. It's like, "Just give me the nice stuff and hold everything that doesn't feel good."

Occasionally we also hear that people just feel overwhelmed by today's world and want church to be a respite from negativity. We're told that by the time Sunday rolls around each week, many church folks feel beaten down by the pressures of life and are only looking for something to soothe their fragmented beings. The church has generally shifted to accommodate this, and besides, haven't we heard it's a new millennium anyway? And all that negative talk about demonic powers, especially here in America, is just so outdated anyway, isn't it?

Death by Church Growth?

In our churches and theological institutions alike, books, DVDs, and classes abound from today's church growth gurus on how to build and grow what they consider a successful church. Many of these experts maintain that if growth is to be achieved, then "positive" messages are mandatory and that some topics are taboo. Certainly, spiritual warfare is on the "no-no" list of many of the growth experts because what it represents would be considered a "negative," as are any other issues dealing with the Devil. But should church growth alone be our goal? Whatever happened to faithfully preaching the whole counsel of God's Word? Has growth become our new master? Is just filling the seats on Sunday the new objective of the church? If so, it is now sadly apparent that reducing the message presented to what is deemed acceptable in the culture has become the means to that objective. It is then also clear that those leading many congregations have indeed lost their moorings.

To avoid the preaching and teaching of doctrine because it's not popular, or the study of eschatology and the end times because some perceive it to be scary, or instruction on spiritual warfare because the existence of Satan is acknowledged in the process, is to ignore enormous portions of Scripture. In fact, to attempt such spiritual gymnastics one must nearly formulate a completely different gospel altogether! The question needs to be asked, is it the church's mission to please the culture or are we beholden to follow the Bible? The correct answer should be obvious, but it's not at all clear that it is.

Today's so-called "feel-good" preaching doesn't threaten Satan in the least. Such themes rarely equip Christians to see captives set free or to win the lost. Telling people merely what they'd *like* to hear on Sunday does little to prepare them to be victors when the Enemy comes knocking. In fact, this is exactly what the apostle Paul warned about in 2 Timothy 4:3-4.

Christianity isn't (or shouldn't be) just about numbers. In fact, in essence it's really not even about humans per se, but about God and His command to make sound disciples who understand what they believe and why (Matthew 28:19-20).

Much more could be stated here, but as we said before, you *are* in a war whether you like it or not, and regardless of how much any church leaders may care to ignore it.

The World, the Flesh, and the Devil

The reason some people are uncomfortable listening to teaching that exposes Satan, his lies, and his works is probably rooted in one of these three areas. Once we identify and discuss these three venues that the Devil operates in, we can better understand which areas need our attention.

First, the world's system scoffs at the reality of a real creature named Satan. It is understandable that those living outside the walls of the Christian faith would talk of the Devil only in jest or use his image as a character to be portrayed at Halloween. While the world would naturally skew any reference to the

Devil, one would think that the church would have a more accurate impression of him. However, with the encroachment of modernism (liberalism) in the church over the past century, we find many people, even in good Bible-believing churches, who hold to extra-biblical ideas about Lucifer.

In truth, Satan is as real today as when Jesus battled with him in the fourth chapter of Luke. He is a tangible, finite being with a very real, finite army. He is focused on his objective and is formidable as a foe, no matter what those in the world may say or believe. So it would seem that the world's view of the Devil has infiltrated our Christian view and watered down reality, a great strategy for Satan to employ, no doubt. Tragically, many in the church have reduced Satan to a myth and diminished the prevalence of demonic powers to something that only the residents of some distant land need to be concerned with.

Our flesh has a natural aversion to accepting the reality of a devil. In fact, we see no way for our humanity to reason out and accept the existence of the supernatural world without the Spirit of God or the forces of hell intervening. Our humanity struggles with comprehending the unseen world, its inhabitants, and the battle for our souls. When it comes to sickness, destruction, poverty, and all of the evil actions of men, most people see only the effects and deny that the cause is rooted in the kingdom of darkness.

With our worldly senses in control, many wrestle with the reality of a spirit world existing at all. For if something can't be touched, tasted, smelled, or experienced by our flesh in some way, then it may just be fantasy and has no basis for concern. Yet millions have overcome this by examining the evidence of who Jesus Christ said He was and what history bears out that He did. That is, the supernatural God of the universe came to earth as a man, died to pay for our unrighteousness, and rose from the grave, and He now calls us to be His own. Praise the Lord!

Another obstacle for many to overcome is the question that if there is a spirit realm, then does evil actually exist in it? In a day when millions have adopted New Age and occult philosophies and practices, an exploding interest has arisen in the supernatural, its powers, and its beings. Ironically, those seeking spiritual experiences outside the bounds of Scripture almost universally deny that any evil beings exist. They believe a trip into the New Age, spiritism, or psychic power is just another way to tap the "goodness" of the universe, which is continually advertised by its seekers as benign and void of harmful inhabitants.

Bible believers caution that *Satan himself is transformed into an angel of light,* but New Age followers have fallen into his trap (2 Corinthians 11:14). Many believe in the powerful and seductive experiences Satan offers, not realizing their blissful acceptance will someday turn tragic. Still others have grasped the reality of Satan's evil powers and have willingly enslaved themselves to his bondage. Regardless, the spirit world is not a fantasyland, and serious consequences will occur if we choose the wrong path into the supernatural.

The world system is constantly pressuring us, mocking the Bible and its presentation about Satan. Likewise, our flesh must continually deal with living in the natural world and resist the temptation to react in kind. And of course, Satan himself wants us to be deceived or confused about his existence, identity, and goals. Ultimately, he wants us to question that he, his demons, and the fallen angels are a factual reality and their driving goal is to steal, kill, and destroy (John 10:10).

Humans, as we've pointed out before, even Christians, are under continual bombardment from the spirit world. Our minds can be fertile playing fields for the powers of darkness. Even the praying Christian who is hiding God's Word in his heart regularly (Psalm 119:11) can be subject to the injection of ideas, confusion, fear, and a host of other thoughts that did not come from God or from their own memory banks. Satan's fiery darts can inflict and influence the believer if there is room to do so.

We know that some will reject this notion; however, countless Christians attest to this reality and many more exhibit lives disrupted by the encroachment of demonic power. In fact, the battles we face and the attacks we endure can be viewed as personal proof that we are indeed in a spiritual war. How odd, though, that anyone could deny that something evil is at work apart from the fallen nature of mankind, when the evidence of such a war permeates our surroundings every day through murder, hatred, strife, and death.

James, Peter, Matthew, Mark, John, and Jude all allude to the spiritual battle as they write, but no man used by God to author the New Testament details spiritual warfare as frequently as Paul does. The apostle Paul knew what it was like to have his peers turn against him for what he believed. He experienced the heartbreak of having his message rejected and his life threatened. Moreover, he knew personally about Satan's attempts to disrupt his preaching, evangelism, travels, and personal life. In the following passages, we see the work of Satan as he fights Paul. From these Scriptures alone it seems impossible for anyone to claim the title of "Christian" and yet deny the authenticity of spiritual warfare, let alone the existence of Satan himself.

> *Wherefore we would have come unto you, even I Paul, once and again; but Satan hindered us.*
> – 1 Thessalonians 2:18

> *And lest I should be exalted above measure through the abundance of the revelations, there was given to me a thorn in the flesh, the messenger of Satan to buffet me, lest I should be exalted above measure.*
> – 2 Corinthians 12:7

Satan Ignored

Some church members, who have been in church all of their lives, still believe that we simply shouldn't discuss the Devil. They prefer to just leave him alone. Others believe that he's no big deal and a waste of breath and time. Perhaps some who have bought into these and other non-biblical views have just never been educated about what Scripture says, or perhaps they just don't want to know.

Within months of being saved, through the diligence of a Christian marriage counselor, I (Eric) recognized that there was a spiritual war going on. Having come from a background as a secular musician and record producer who was addicted to drugs and had come straight out of the New Age movement, I became acutely aware of the conflict in the spiritual realm. Attending a church in our neighborhood in Seattle, my wife and I came face to face with apathetic, liberal Christianity. Each Sunday the pastor would ask if anything good had happened to anyone that week – what most of us would refer to as a time of testimony.

By this point in my walk with God, I was feeling the call of God to ministry and had grown in boldness. I knew that many of the folks surrounding me in the pews each Sunday had never had the same kind of life-changing experience with Jesus Christ that I delighted in. With this in mind, and to the chagrin of those seated near me, I immediately raised my hand nearly every time the pastor called for testimonies. One Sunday I stood and exclaimed how blessed Melanie and I were that God had delivered us from the kingdom of darkness, broken Satan's grip, and made us a part of His family. The "amens" were few that day. After church, one of the elders of the church approached me in the foyer and commented, "Eric, I don't know why you talk about the Devil so much. He never affects me."

Perhaps if I had known then just a portion of what I

understand now, I would have said, "Well, sir, that's because you are no threat to his kingdom!"

Satan Empowered

Conversely, many in the church today lend too much attention to and ascribe too much power to Satan. This is just as unhealthy as trying to ignore him. Some folks believe he is given nearly equal status with our Lord, and we are no match for him. Some believe that if they talk about the Devil, he's going to get them. They claim that coming into conflict with him is like spreading honey on hot tin – it's going to attract flies, and they just don't want to deal with it.

Perhaps they are right about confrontation attracting attention. For sure, those who decide to do what is right and follow the leading of Scripture may endure some attacks, but that's just part of living the Christian life. However, since when does the Devil abide by any sort of Geneva Convention rules anyway? Warfare is a fact of life and everyone – EVERYONE – is either winning or losing. Those who think they can be conscientious objectors in spiritual warfare have already abdicated their potential victory.

No one has ever correctly stated that living the Christian life was going to be stress and pain free or simple and easy. Scripture never teaches that. Also, it doesn't say, "Ignore the Devil and he'll ignore you." No, the Bible instructs us to take a stand; resist the Devil, his workers, and his power; and then watch as God runs him out of town (James 4:7b). What a great assurance we have – if we'll just follow the Word!

Playing into the Devil's Hands

Another sobering factor emerges besides ignoring Satan or fearing him, and that is ignorance. Ignorance of the spirit realm, its inhabitants, their activities, their abilities, and spiritual warfare in general is without a doubt one of Satan's best tools in leading to the breakdown of righteousness and powerful Christian living. Ignorance has also aided the encroachment of liberalism within Christian ranks over the last century in particular.

Clearly, the Bible states that there will be some among us who are merely along for the ride. These "Christians," using the term very loosely, accept and enjoy the nice and pleasant things about Christianity, but when it comes to the stuff of spiritual warfare, the Devil, and obedience to the Word of God, they cannot stand firm. Jesus referred to these people when He said, *Not every one that saith unto me, Lord, Lord, shall enter into the kingdom of heaven; but he that doeth the will of my Father which is in heaven* (Matthew 7:21). To these uninformed and mostly unsaved people, Christianity is viewed primarily as a social club, and the church building as a gathering place to make an appearance on Sunday. Instead, Christians should be an army engaged in a war, and the church a training ground to help equip the soldiers, and a hospital to bind up those wounded in the conflict.

Who's Afraid of the Devil?

Contrary to the belief of many, not one verse in the Bible tells the Christian to fear the Devil. We are on the winning side! First Peter 1:5 points out that because we have faith in the Lord, we are shielded by the power of God from Satan's wrath. Otherwise, we would surely meet destruction at the hands of the Evil One. How wonderful to know that those covered in Christ's precious blood are *more than conquerors through him that loved us* (Romans 8:37). Victors in Christ! Yes, soldiers on the winning side!

Instead of nervously trembling in fear of the Devil, the Bible says, *The fear of the Lord is the beginning of knowledge* (Proverbs 1:7). This does not mean that God's people should fear Him as a child fears a cruel or abusive parent. Though God is a righteous God and will judge the living and the dead, He is also the God of love who desires the very best for His own. In fact, the Hebrew word translated "fear" in Proverbs 1:7 is *yirah*, which means "reverence." We should hold an awesome, loving, holy reverence for the Lord, and yes, if our lives are consumed with sin and strife, we should fear Him.

Satan often operates from the position of our ignorance. As a matter of course, he is also freed to varying extents if we choose to be disobedient in following God's Word and allow sin to gain a foothold in our lives and homes. With that in mind, we know that if the fear of the Lord is the beginning of knowledge and wisdom, then the fear of the Devil must be the beginning of ignorance. For the believer, showing ignorance by fearing Satan surely furthers his mission to rival God. It is that simple. We need to have a healthy fear toward God, not the Devil. So, ask yourself, "Whom do I fearfully enthrone in my heart?"

Every time an angel of the Lord appeared to men, the Bible tells us, the first thing the angel always said was, "Fear not. Don't be afraid of me. Fear the almighty God." We see this truth repeated all through Scripture. But fear was the first emotion that Satan used to turn the heart of man away from God. Remember, in the garden, Adam said, *I heard thy voice in the garden, and I was afraid* (Genesis 3:10). The Bible tells us to fear God, not to fear the Devil. Nevertheless, Satan's manipulation of fear continues to this day.

Being pensive or fearful of the unknown is a natural human reaction. Though explorers see the unknown as a horizon to be crossed or a new vista to be charted, this "spirit" is not the norm. History proves how rare this breed of man or woman really is. Most of us become set in our ways in this life and try to work around excursions into uncharted waters. Satan often capitalizes on this human trait as he methodically plans his attacks on our lives and homes. He is counting on people being fearful through their own ignorance of him.

Most of us would simply rather not deal with the unknown. This flaw in human nature leads us to shy away from learning about or dealing with whatever it is we don't understand. Satan loves to see Christians operate in ignorance because he knows that biblically literate believers, empowered by the cross and led by God's Word, are going to be a formidable foe to him. But those walking in ignorance are no match for his deceptions. In fact, he knows that believers who lack understanding and training in God's army are sitting ducks, prey for his minions to taunt and to bind. The Devil must be particularly fond of those Christians who consciously refuse to resist him.

Speaking of believers, the Bible says, *for we are not ignorant of his [Satan's] devices* (2 Corinthians 2:11b). The immediate reaction by some is, "I'm not stupid. I know what's going on." But the Bible never calls us stupid. The Word of God warns the saints about being without knowledge of the workings of the Enemy. That is ignorance, not stupidity, and there is a difference.

But Satan Can't Hurt Me

> *Lest Satan should get an advantage of us: for we are not ignorant of his devices.* – 2 Corinthians 2:11

The first part of 2 Corinthians 2:11 points out the very real possibility that the lives of believers can be interrupted by the powers of darkness. This idea runs contrary to much preaching we hear today. The rationalization being proclaimed in many circles is, "Just be a good Christian and you'll have nothing to worry about." Oh, if it were really that simple!

Without getting into the argument of whether a Christian can actually be possessed by a demon or not, this passage alone makes it obvious that we, and our homes, can be affected by demonic intruders. *Lest Satan should get an advantage of us.* Sadly, many choose ignorance in the arena of spiritual warfare. The costs of this unwise decision are lives, families, and churches in spiritual disarray and defeat.

When ministering on this in my seminars, I (David) use the analogy that ignorance is driving thirty-five miles an hour in a twenty-five-mile-an-hour zone and not knowing what the speed limit is. When the police officer pulls you over, the first thing he says is, "Do you know how fast you were going?"

When you answer, "Well, I didn't know the speed limit here," does the officer say, "I'm sorry. There was a sign just back down the road. I thought everyone saw it. You are probably in a hurry. I'll just let you go"? Is that how they do it? No. You are responsible to know the law. Not knowing is ignorance.

Stupidity, on the other hand, is knowing that the speed limit is twenty-five miles an hour and doing thirty-five miles an hour while waving at the police officer as you pass him. That's stupidity.

More than Ignorance

We wonder just how many Christians are uneasy with a discussion like this. As we've pointed out, a common misconception is to leave well enough alone. But a good soldier involved in a good fight can't just leave his adversary alone, especially when that soldier understands the ultimate importance of his mission, both to himself and to those he has been given charge over. Therefore, understanding may be the key to victory in the battle.

Hosea 4:6 states: *My people are destroyed for lack of knowledge: because thou hast rejected knowledge, I will also reject thee, that thou shalt be no priest to me: seeing thou hast forgotten the law of thy God, I will also forget thy children.* Let that sink in.

How often we have heard this passage recited and preached, yet the keys to this discussion may be found in its words.

We don't understand what God has clearly outlined in Scripture.

We go out of our way to avoid finding knowledge, rejecting His call to get wisdom and understanding (Proverbs 2:2).

Then we wonder why our priestly authority seems powerless, and we are dismayed at how easily our children go out to follow other gods.

Without a doubt, one of the root causes of the anemic level of victory for many in the church today is ignorance about the constant spiritual barrage being waged against us. We desperately need to bone up in this area. Congregations find themselves ineffective in their witness and walk for Christ, while families are splintered and often in tragic disarray as they face the Enemy without a knowledge of spiritual warfare.

Perhaps many who have been beaten down by the adversary's attacks have merely opted to accept a level of spiritual victory far below what they are entitled to as believers. While perfectly capable of attaining victory, these saints are failing because of their lack of knowledge. This ignorance breeds fear about the tools and methods of the Enemy and skews a proper biblical view of the arena of spiritual warfare. The result: Satan wins. Just imagine where you, your family, and your church would be if everyone involved would grasp the power of God's Word, act on it, and reach for the higher ground in our experience with God. Talk about joy unspeakable and full of glory!

He's Gonna Get Ya!

The Bible tells us not to be ignorant of Satan's devices, yet people unwittingly warn us against carrying out the ministries of exposing the Devil and his schemes. They do so out of fear, supposing that the Devil is going to get anyone who meddles in his affairs. To believe that the Devil hates you any more or is out to get you any more than he previously was because of what you do is a misconception. He is out to destroy anyone and everyone possible. Though he may temporarily increase the intensity of an attack on a person, we need to keep in mind that the Devil instinctively hates people because of who we are – human beings in God's creation – not what we do.

Blinded, ineffective, frightened, and unaware humans make it easy for Satan to accomplish his purposes. Fearing demonic retaliation in reciprocation for any righteous action we take is the pinnacle of Satan's intimidation at work. It's kind of like the Mafia wanting protection payments from you, although they know that they've run out of bullets and can only operate on the fearful perceptions that people have of them. To be intimidated by his power because we don't understand it is exactly what Satan wants. To walk in the power, purpose, and knowledge of the Holy Spirit, while understanding the limitations of the Enemy is exactly what God wants for us. You will make the decision as to which way you and your family will go.

We Are Ambassadors

Perhaps the most powerful information Christians can possess is the sure understanding of who they are in Jesus Christ. Though our position in Him could be the subject of an entire book, the passage below powerfully and simply illustrates it.

> *Now then we are ambassadors for Christ, as though God did beseech you by us: we pray you in Christ's stead, be ye reconciled to God. For he hath made him to be sin for us, who knew no sin; that we might be made the righteousness of God in him.*
> – 2 Corinthians 5:20-21

Here Paul makes a fervent appeal to the Corinthians to fall

on the mercy of God and realize the great salvation available to them through Christ's atonement. In doing so, he refers to himself and others accompanying him as ambassadors. This speaks to those who are mature in Christ, having left the "milk" or infancy of the faith, and who now enjoy the "meat" of a rich, deep relationship with God.

The actual word *ambassadors* used here comes from the Greek word *Presbuteros*, which is where the word *presbytery* originates. It is interchangeable in the New Testament with the words *elder*, *bishop*, and *overseer*. But what catches our eye is the proclamation here that Paul and others are called *ambassadors*.

Noted English Bible scholar and eighteenth-century pastor Dr. John Gill commented: "Since God has made reconciliation by Christ, and the ministry of it is committed to us, we are ambassadors for him; we come with full powers from him." Indeed, "full powers." Praise the Lord!

Webster's Dictionary states: "Ambassador, Embassador: 1. A minister of the highest rank sent to a foreign court to represent there his sovereign or country; 2. An official messenger and representative."

When the president of the United States appoints an ambassador to Canada, he bestows upon said ambassador the weight and responsibility to act on behalf of the United States and its affairs inside the country of Canada. The only occasion in which the ambassador relinquishes his absolute-yet-controlled powers would be when the president himself comes and sets foot on Canadian soil. The same is true of Christians. According to Scripture, we are ambassadors of the kingdom of God. Until our Commander-in-Chief comes and sets His foot here on earth, He has left us the instructions on how to carry out His wishes as we walk in complete ambassadorship. We have ultimate authority as we operate on behalf of the kingdom of God and come in Jesus' name.

If indeed we are His ambassadors, our mission must be to clearly present the unabashed gospel to a lost and dying world. But along with carrying out the Great Commission (Matthew 28:19-20), we need to understand that since Jesus came to destroy the powers of darkness (1 John 3:8), we must carry on the enforcement of His triumph with great confidence and vigor while taking direct aim against the Devil's kingdom.

We Are Conquerors

This leads us from being ambassadors, endowed with every authority of His throne, to being conquerors over sin, hell, and the grave.

Paul admonishes the Romans to realize their position in Christ when he states: *we are more than conquerors through him that loved us* (Romans 8:37).

Jesus instructs us here about the authority bestowed upon the believer:

> *Behold, I give unto you power to tread on serpents*
> *and scorpions, and over all the power of the enemy:*
> *and nothing shall by any means hurt you.*
> – Luke 10:19

It is clear, isn't it? We are more than conquerors, aren't we? Either we are and Jesus was right, or we aren't and He was wrong. Can there be any middle ground? No! Jesus surely didn't come and give His life so we could proclaim that we're "kinda" conquerors some of the time. The reality we need to start living in is that we are more than conquerors all of the time – even when times are tough and the going is hard. When the church realizes its position, authority, and role in Him, and takes seriously the call to disarm the powers of darkness, we'll move in the realm in which He ordained us to operate.

And having disarmed the powers and authorities,

*he made a public spectacle of them, triumphing over
them by the cross.*
– Colossians 2:15 (NIV)

*Giving thanks unto the Father, which hath made us
meet to be partakers of the inheritance of the saints
in light: Who hath delivered us from the power of
darkness, and hath translated us into the kingdom of his dear Son: In whom we have redemption
through his blood, even the forgiveness of sins.*
– Colossians 1:12-14

What a joy in knowing that, no matter where we've come from
or how low our lives may have once been, as Christians we're
now conquering ambassadors for the kingdom of God!

Chapter 3

Fruitful Warfare

But the fruit of the Spirit is love, joy, peace, longsuf-
fering, gentleness, goodness, faith, Meekness, tem-
perance: against such there is no law.
– Galatians 5:22-23

Is the Devil Mad at You?

D o you realize why biblical followers of Christ are in control of their emotions? Do you know why their lives
are not filled with anger, hatred, unrest, and other evil qualities? It is because the fruit of the Holy Spirit – love, joy, peace,
longsuffering (patience), gentleness, kindness, meekness, and
temperance – is working in their lives.

Undoubtedly, these biblical fruits suppress anger, bitterness,
hatred, and malice in the lives of believers. This also illustrates a
microcosm of the battle in the spiritual realm: evil versus good;
right versus wrong; love versus hate; the fruits of the Spirit of
God versus those of the Prince of Darkness.

In preparing for spiritual warfare, we must comprehend

that the Devil is totally and completely void of the qualities represented by God's fruit. Indeed, realizing this helps us define the battle lines and the adversary's tactics. We are empowered by remembering that there is nothing we can do to upset the Evil One. Satan's work is the very reason people get upset in the first place. He is already upset, bitter, hate filled, and enraged beyond any human imagination. He is the Evil One. Therefore, any actions we take are not going to make him any angrier. He's already angry and we cannot increase or decrease that anger one bit. No steps taken against the kingdom of darkness can increase his desire to see us fail; he wants us destroyed. Yet the paralyzing fearfulness generated by this misconception is a genuine detriment to being released to victorious spiritual living.

We are aware that this runs counter to what many Christians have either been taught or merely perceived as they have gone to Sunday school. However, believing a misconception doesn't make it any less accurate or less biblical. Thinking otherwise ascribes to Satan ability and power outside what Scripture outlines. Let's look at this further.

Satan Happy?

In referring to some instance or event, we often hear Christians say, "Well, that ought to make Satan happy." How can that be? Though people are merely pointing out some event or circumstance where Satan has gained a foothold or an advantage, we should understand that nothing actually makes him happy. Our lack of biblical action is not going to make him happy either. It is impossible for Satan to be happy. He once understood and experienced the greatness and beauty of God as one of God's key servants. And though he may truly believe his own deception (that he, a finite being, can eventually conquer God Almighty), he does have access to the total revelation of what

God proclaims his future fate is. Read here as God speaks to Satan in Ezekiel 28:14-16:

> *Thou art the anointed cherub that covereth; and I have set thee so: thou wast upon the holy mountain of God; thou hast walked up and down in the midst of the stones of fire. Thou wast perfect in thy ways from the day that thou wast created, till iniquity was found in thee. By the multitude of thy merchandise they have filled the midst of thee with violence, and thou hast sinned: therefore I will cast thee as profane out of the mountain of God: and I will destroy thee.*

The Great Intimidator: Why Many Don't Fight

When discussing the spirit realm, we need to consider the idea that our human emotions concerning evil and good are also available to the Enemy and his troops. While it is true that Satan manipulates emotions like fear, intimidation, and pain to accomplish his mission in human lives, he is at best limited and perhaps void of any degree of emotion as we know it. He knows that most humans know little about spiritual warfare and thus will take the bait and buy into what he is selling. It works and has done so for about six thousand years, so why change now? He sets up scenarios that play human emotions like a piano, and watches people react without faith, allowing an even bigger foothold on their lives for the powers of darkness to operate.

We know that if Satan is devoid of emotions and feelings, then those in the spirit realm under Satan's command will exhibit few emotions – perhaps none – as well. Could theirs be any more than a cut-and-dried, antiseptic existence, driven by the hopelessness and bondage of Satan himself? While it is much more dynamic and interesting to portray the workers of darkness as raging, seething creatures, any such facade only veils the cold, calculating, and focused mission they are enslaved by their master to follow.

Though we often express our love for the Lord through the praise of our lips and should constantly find ourselves in an attitude of worship and adoration toward Him, the same is not true of Satan worshipers. Though they pay homage to their master with words and through ritual activities, few worship the Devil with real heartfelt thanks, weeping for joy that they know him. Certainly, no classical Satan worshiper, who understands whom he follows, feels any love in his heart at midnight on Halloween.

Conversely, the fact that almighty God sent His Son to save us from our sins regularly brings many of us to our knees, joyfully worshiping Him with every fiber of our being. Perhaps the only exception to this line of reasoning will be the false worship presented to the Antichrist during the tribulation period in the last days (Revelation 13:3). Scripture reveals that people around the globe will genuinely and tragically give glory to this counterfeit Christ. In those days, Satan will actually be receiving adoration, for through his earthly representative, he will be glorified as deceived mankind follows him to their destruction.

Truly, the Devil has no ability to possess love, joy, peace, longsuffering, or any other fruit of the Holy Spirit. Quite the opposite is true. While we humans may vacillate from time to time in the degree that these fruits operate and are apparent in us, Satan is 100 percent evil, 100 percent of the time. He's the meanest of mean dudes and he can't do anything to change. He is the epitome of fear and terror, and nothing we do will increase the degree to which these characteristics are manifest. He will maintain the same hateful attitude toward us regardless of what we do.

But when we engage in spiritual warfare, fighting the good fight, we take back ground otherwise lost to the powers of darkness through our ignorance of their powers and activities. Scriptural action – that is, warfare – nullifies the will of the adversary. Praise the Lord! If emotions were possible for him, the Devil and his workers would sense discouragement when they come upon a Christian filled with God's Spirit, knowledgeable of His Word, prepared for battle, and ready for action.

Resist

Since the powers of darkness are not infinite, we gain a great advantage when we realize that acts of spiritual warfare actually weaken future attacks. This is what the apostle James is speaking of in James 4:7: *Submit yourselves therefore to God. Resist the devil, and he will flee from you.*

The Greek word translated *resist* here is *antitassomai,* which literally means "to oppose" and "to range oneself against something." Our position can never be neutral. This passage certainly encourages Christians to assume an offensive posture – not simply one of defense or abstinence.

Resisting the Devil begins with our pledge of obedience to God's Word by a life dedicated to walking in the fruit of the Spirit; it is solidified by the acts of spiritual warfare against the powers of darkness. We must start with having a working understanding of the Enemy's camp.

Rule number one in resisting the Evil One is to remember that we are engaged in a constant battle that will cease only when the Lord Jesus comes again. We may be intimidated, but if we persevere, the victory is ours. And because we have exhibited our strength in God, demonic powers will eventually move on to a more unsuspecting prey to accomplish their mission. Resisting the Devil does work, and we really are more than conquerors. Wow!

So, to view the spirit realm and our role as believers correctly, the notion that "ignorance is bliss" and other misconceptions about spiritual warfare must be dealt with in our hearts and minds. While it is true that engaging in spiritual warfare may sometimes seem to acquire the wrath of the Devil, that's not the case. When we expose Satan (Ephesians 5:11) and when we resist him (James 4:7), he may indeed turn up the heat. He may throw an increased amount of his spiritual and even physical junk at us, try to give the impression that he is invincible, and attempt to make us believe that we are no match.

However, our spiritual struggle only becomes more focused and brings an increased awareness as the Enemy attacks and counterattacks. Most likely, an upturn in the battle means that we are being effective or Satan senses that victory for us is imminent. His methods may seem more devious, his attacks seemingly more potent, and their effects or oppression on our hearts and minds may feel more painful or unsettling; but rest assured, if we don't give up, he will not win. If we remain focused and scriptural, he cannot win!

As good soldiers, we are merely following our Commander. Upon sensing Satan's increased attacks, we will also have real and tangible evidence that we are engaged in a war because our Enemy is exhibiting signs that we are being effective through the power of the cross. This evidence will bode well and help us build spiritual muscle as we endeavor to take even more territory for the kingdom of God.

On the other hand, being fearful of or simply ignoring God's call to pick up the weapons of spiritual warfare and engage in the battle will assure that Satan attains at least a partial victory in any given situation. Why give him that? God has done His part, now we must do ours. Once again, James 4:7 instructs us to *resist the Devil*. This is not optional. The same verse promises that if we do resist him, *he will flee*. The image is one of a fleeing army, scattered in battle after a merciless defeat. Satan is to be crushed under our feet, for Scripture teaches that he is under the foot of the Savior. Don't let him up!

When Satan brings out the "big guns," remember that God has a bigger one. When we feel overwhelmed in the spiritual struggles we encounter, remember, the battle is the Lord's (2 Chronicles 20:15). The Lord is our fortress in times of trouble (Psalm 71:3). Scripture assures us that under His wings there is refuge, as He has commissioned angels to assist and guard us (Psalm 91:11). Praise His name!

Satan's Intimidation: The Fear Factor

When people understand that this book teaches about and against the Devil, some will reject it because of their private fear of him. Without even bothering to read it, some will throw out the old excuse, "Oh, Benoit and Barger are just too far out ... they see demons everywhere ... they teach that scary stuff ...." And others will have no interest because they can't relate to the topic of spiritual warfare. Often, lack of basic understanding on issues leads us to miss the very things we need a good dose of teaching on.

Yet, if these pages were to talk only of the attributes of God, the same syndrome could occur. Sadly, if this were a work about the character of God, who will one day judge the living and the dead, some would ignore it simply because they possess no fear of the Lord. We're talking about an awesome God who created the entire universe and will one day cast the Devil and every demon, fallen angel, and lost soul who rejects His free gift of salvation into eternal darkness. We're talking about the lake of fire and total separation from God's righteous love forever and ever and ever. Get the picture?

Thank God for His wonderful salvation! Yet, somehow some believers – yes, church members – don't fear Him, but instead fear the Devil. It certainly seems upside down, doesn't it? In fact, what has happened is a lack of understanding, a loss of the reality of eternity, and surely no vision for the reverence and awe of God.

More Misconceptions

Greater is he that is in you, than he that is in the world. – 1 John 4:4b

We have heard much talk about witches and Devil worshipers praying against Christians, and occultists praying for the demise of those in Christian ministry. While this is undoubtedly true, we believe their results have been exaggerated. In fact, a reaction of near panic has occurred when some Christians describe these reports. In some circles, the way folks talk about what Satan's human workers are doing and the damage they are allegedly inflicting is akin to superstition.

Now, don't misunderstand. In our ministries we have encountered witches and satanists who have opposed us. Once, several years ago on Halloween weekend, I (Eric) was ministering at Southern Illinois University. I had been asked to come and speak about the occult. My contact from the Baptist Student Union and I were backstage praying as people filed into the auditorium. After I was introduced, I began my presentation, but I felt an unusually strong hindrance, a spiritual blockage.

After fumbling through the first ten minutes of the seminar, I stopped and simply stated that I knew in my spirit that people were present who opposed my ministry and me. I stated that anyone who was actually praying against the presentation should beware; I was rejecting their negative prayers and was sending back the power of God. I was able to declare that because I was protected and ready, shielded by faith and covered by the blood of Jesus, their actions could not and would not stop what the Lord had ordained.

The place erupted in applause – not just a little applause – it was thunderous. Thinking about it now, the length of the applause and its intensity was almost comical. When I resumed my presentation, immediately I had a peace of mind and clarity of speech that was not there minutes earlier. What I didn't know was that while I had been backstage in prayer, the very vocal, high-profile coven of witches on the campus had filed in and was sitting across the entire second row before me. Everybody in the entire building knew it – everyone except me.

How did I know there was opposition and that the hindrance I felt in my thoughts and presentation just wasn't from lack of sleep or the exhaustion of travel? Tiredness and crazy schedules are things we incur regularly in our ministries, but this was different. This was a spiritual battle going on, one that I may not have been sensitive to if I hadn't been in constant and recent communion with God. Though some Christians may be too quick to blame all interferences on the Devil, the sad reality is that far too few believers exercise discernment when facing spiritual opposition. The fact is that without a close and connected walk with God, scriptural understanding, and exercising spiritual discernment, we'll be of no consequence to the forces of wickedness and will do little to disarm the powers of darkness.

There is absolutely no shortcut for a dedicated devotional life. However, the benefits cannot be overstated. It aids us in the entire arena of human life, but it is of utmost importance during times of spiritual struggle and opposition. Otherwise, I might have ineffectively limped through the evening's seminar, and the witches would have gone on their way, declaring a victory over an ineffective and undiscerning preacher.

Were the witches' prayers actually affecting me? Yes, but by following the biblical commands of resisting and exposing what I knew was happening in the spirit realm, I overcame the occult activity. Not only was I able to conduct the seminar in power, speaking effectively with good recall and poise, but God also used the occasion to show Himself strong over the powers of the occultists before several hundred students on that campus.

Could I have missed it? Could I have just fantasized the feelings? Certainly. In our humanity we do sometimes miss it, but if we don't act in concert with the Word of God and in accordance with how we believe the Holy Spirit is leading us, isn't timidity and silence potentially more troublesome and certainly less honoring to the Lord? The fact is, however, that the seminar presentation that was noticeably out of joint as it began ended with a great victory for God. We wonder how many students might have left the witches' coven, or perhaps might have chosen not to join it, when they saw how the power of God overcame the power of witchcraft that night.

Therefore, sensing opposition because of occult manifestations and actually being manipulated because of them are two different things. If a Christian sins, is it because his next-door neighbor is casting a spell on him? No. If a pastor or minister falls, can we blame it all on the work ethic of satanists or occultists? No. Scripture tells us that we are all accountable for our own actions. Our sins are truly our own, and though the work of some third party given over to the powers of darkness may add to the effect, to identify hexes and curses as the *sole* reason for our troubles, sicknesses, or sins does two unhealthy and unscriptural things.

First, by blaming the occult we shirk our own personal responsibility to live a righteous life. Though we are certain to sin, God's keeping power and the strength of Jesus' blood is greater than our sins. Thank God, that if we sin, His forgiveness is available through the power of repentance.

Second, by blaming the occult prayers of others for our actions, we are in effect yielding to the powers of Satan. This attitude surely dethrones the Savior and glorifies the Devil. In this way, God's people ascribe to the Devil more power than the Word of God intimates that he possesses. This says nothing of those who seem to place Satan on an equal level with God. Of all people, we believers are supposed to know what Scripture says, and it never alludes to any such lofty position for the Prince of Darkness. Remember, vainly professing equality with God was Lucifer's intention to start with and the very reason for his eviction from heaven (Isaiah 14:12-15).

Any effect that satanically inspired prayers may have cannot match the effects of prayerlessness and the lack of knowledge about spiritual warfare of many in the church. Make no mistake – occult prayers, spells, and incantations do wield power, but do they really have the ability to single-handedly destroy? With direction from the underworld, these prayers are merely aimed at preexisting weaknesses that may already have a grip on any given man or woman. Isn't it a waste of time to be overly concerned about what the witches might be up to – especially if it becomes an unhealthy or unbiblical fascination?

Our efforts should be concentrated on seeking the Lord, staying washed in His blood, and walking in a manner befitting the calling we have received. Part of that walk is having a healthy, biblical understanding of the arena of spiritual warfare, whether we're involved in full-time ministry or not.

Likewise, many people constantly say we shouldn't talk about the Devil, because then we'll be giving him praise, as if he has a mystical name, never to be uttered. Well, as we've pointed out, the Scripture implores us to expose his works and deeds. When the Scriptures were written, the name of Jehovah was so revered that the scribes changed their pens when they penned the name of Jehovah. Tragically, some people throw

God's name out all over the place, but by their attitude they reverence the name of the Devil. By believing that we should be silent about the Devil's schemes, many allow the door of ignorance to swing open and sometimes slam shut – right on their lives and homes.

Chapter 4

There's Power in the Blood

As we've pointed out, several different views emerge in the church today on the topic and definition of spiritual warfare. We want to make it clear that while we do not agree with the affinity some show in blaming every shortcoming known to man on a direct intervention by demons, we certainly do not want to downplay the importance of recognizing and exposing the work of evil. Neither do we want to discount the validity and severity of the demonic or in any way trivialize the need to help people who are afflicted by Satan's works.

In our public ministries, we have both dealt with demon-possessed people and have seen God triumph over Satan with regularity. And while we don't intend to demean any of those in "deliverance ministries," we'd like to see them all put out of business, and we actually think they would want that as well. Here's why. We question the prevailing attitude in the church today that seems to abdicate its basic responsibility to "set the captives free," as Scripture directs. Every Christian carries the responsibility to be first spiritually prepared and secondly willing to act against the forces of evil when necessary.

We don't go looking for a demonic fight, but if one comes our way, we'll accommodate accordingly. If the saints were prepared, educated about such things, and prayerful, wouldn't exposing and expelling evil forces be the normal course of action? No matter which camp you might be from, we believe that we can all agree that personal victory is a mandatory and most basic step to take. But before we can assist others on the road to freedom, how do we go about defeating the Devil and his forces in our own lives?

The Power of the Blood

The most important element in our personal victory is a clear, biblical understanding of the blood of Jesus Christ. Knowing what the blood has done, is doing, and will do for us is essential if we are to comprehend Christ's magnificence and overwhelming ability to save, heal, and deliver. Scripture tells us that Jesus' going to the cross and shedding His blood for us accomplished many different things.

Hebrews 9:14 assures us that the blood of the Lamb has the power to cleanse us.

Ephesians 1:7 says that the blood brings forgiveness.

Romans 5:9 teaches that Christ's blood sacrifice justifies us.

Colossians 1:14 and Hebrews 9:12 declare that we are redeemed by the power of His precious blood.

Colossians 1:20 tells us that lasting peace comes by the blood.

1 John 1:7 indicates that we are purified through it.

Revelation 1:5 speaks of the complete freedom believers enjoy as the blood of Jesus washes us and separates us from our sins.

Revelation 5:9 reveals the monumental truth that there was but one thing that could purchase mankind's freedom and allow us fellowship with God once more – the blood of His only Son!

The blood represents a lasting testimony that eternal God loved mankind so much that He sent His only Son to pay the price for their sins and to redeem them from the curse of death, hell, and the grave. Alleluia! We are allowed redemption because of faith in Christ and His sacrifice through the shedding of His blood. Nothing more and nothing less can save us.

Though the blood of Jesus Christ represents many wonderful things, His shed blood also achieves the once-for-all defeat of Satan and eternal freedom for all who will believe. We can rest in the knowledge that if the blood of Jesus sealed Satan's doom, it was certainly enough to seal us in God. Theologians call that efficacious. We call it wonderful. Furthermore, Christ's blood is not gone, dead, or dried up on the dirt of Golgotha. The power hasn't disintegrated since that dark afternoon two thousand years ago when He hung on a cross for all mankind. It's alive, powerful, and available for every saint of God today – not just as doctrine but also as a weapon of victorious warfare.

The Recipe for Victory

And they overcame him by the blood of the Lamb, and by the word of their testimony; and they loved not their lives unto the death.
– Revelation 12:11

Beloved, listen carefully. We are going to refer to the above passage several times in the coming pages because your ultimate victory over the powers of darkness depends on it. You could read all the books, listen to all the tapes and CDs, and learn all that has ever been taught on spiritual warfare and yet never win. Unless you apply what you know by turning your learning into action, you have accomplished nothing. For sure, the Devil will do just about anything to deter you from first examining and then acting on what this potent passage in Revelation 12 tells us.

Excitement grows as we see that God has laid out a surefire battle plan for His children to follow. The simple formula is understandable, and the victory attainable if we'll just do it. This passage is a definite key – even more important than the many other passages that we've quoted in our review of spiritual warfare. In this futuristic passage, the path to success is given to us. Read it. Learn it. Quote it. Believe it!

Here in Revelation 12:11, *they* refers to the saints of God – us. The *him* here is the Devil. *They overcame him.* But how? *By the blood of the Lamb, and by the word of their testimony.* Granted, this verse is from the book of Revelation, which is perhaps the most controversial and misunderstood of the sixty-six different books or letters that comprise the Bible. Revelation is speaking of a future struggle, and though some may argue that the depiction here is only a onetime historical event predicted in Scripture, the relevancy of this passage to us today is crucial. Though the interpretations of the book of Revelation and this chapter in particular may vary, this passage seems to stand out as a universal battle cry for the saints of God.

It is interesting that verse 10 depicts Satan being cast out of heaven, and verse 4 portrays the rebellious angels (one-third of the total) that followed Satan and were banished from God's presence and cast down to earth. These events chronologically precede Adam and Eve, let alone our day. We see Christ recounting that He saw Satan fall from heaven as lightning in Luke 10:18. He is speaking as if it were already done (indeed, it was done before time as we know it). So it is safe to assume that our key verse (v. 11) is itself a universal truth and not just a onetime historical event.

Biblical chronology aside, we can rest in the fact that the blood of Jesus Christ is without question the most potent element in the Christian's fight against evil. Without it, we are doomed, still lost in our sins, and heading for hell. Christ's blood is the one primary ingredient that makes or breaks Christianity, for Christianity minus the blood of Jesus becomes just another worthless religion with no eternal significance on the landscape of planet Earth.

Early in my (Eric) walk with God, I learned the outright horror that demons have for the blood of Jesus Christ. Like many Christians, I had the general understanding of what the blood had accomplished for me in salvation. However, an unforgettable event took place around 1985 that highlighted the power of the blood of the Lamb and the effect it has in the spirit realm.

My wife, Melanie, and I had driven with several friends from our home (then in Bellingham, Washington) to Vancouver, Canada, to attend a radio rally being held by an American evangelist with whom I had become acquainted. After the rally, with the large hall nearly empty, we were waiting to greet my friend, the evangelist. As we waited, I noticed him talking with a teenage girl. Though the conversation was indistinguishable and no one else seemed to notice, it became obvious that my friend was dealing with a problem of a serious nature.

Suddenly and without notice, the girl violently attacked the evangelist, picking him up with one hand by the throat. I bolted across the foyer of the building and attempted to restrain the girl, but with little success. She continued to hold my friend by the throat, and though I attempted to pull her free, she dragged us across the foyer where she commenced beating the evangelist against the wall. Finally, help arrived, and they quickly went to work binding the multiple demons that possessed her.

During the deliverance session, which lasted over two hours, we learned some very powerful spiritual lessons. The girl had been involved in satanic sacrifices and had willed her soul to Satan. (Over the ensuing weeks, more information came out as my pastor and I dealt with her and the many emotional and spiritual problems that arose from her involvement in satanism.) As the evangelist ministered to her, three others, myself included, restrained her and prayed for God's delivering power. During the deliverance session, the evangelist held a Bible in front of the girl's face, but the demons reacted violently. When he commanded, "In the name of Jesus," the spirit(s) possessing her reacted again. But when the evangelist said, "By the authority of the blood of Jesus Christ," the demon-possessed girl broke free and had to be tackled.

The lesson learned that night is important to us today. Though Satan wants no part of the Bible and he knows that the name of Jesus spells his doom, the authority of the blood of Jesus Christ, being applied by a knowledgeable ambassador of God, is the most potent weapon in the Christian's spiritual arsenal, bar none. Demons are powerless against the blood. Satan cannot penetrate the blood. Wherever the blood is, Satan's power is neutralized. Amen! So then, how do we utilize or apply the blood of Christ since there is no actual physical blood? Looking at the Old Testament, to see what the Israelites did at the time of the Exodus, will give us insight for our lives today.

Where the Blood Meets the Hyssop

The Old Testament comes alive with rich, fertile teaching when the physical examples and stories are paralleled in a spiritual sense for New Testament believers today. The account of the exodus is rich with the use of *types* (also called typologies) for us to learn from. Here we see God's plan finally take shape to spring His people, Israel, from their burdensome captivity. Israel had been captive, slaves to Pharaoh year after year, just as humans without Jesus are captives of Satan, enslaved to sin.

The story of the Jewish captivity in Egypt both parallels human captivity to evil and pictures spiritual warfare in a powerful way. Repeatedly, Moses had cried out to the Egyptian king, "Let my people go!" and over and over, the answer was no. One miraculous sign after another came and went, and still Pharaoh was unrelenting because his heart was hardened. The king had seen Moses throw dust into the air, and it became the plague of boils over the land. Aaron's staff had devoured those of the sorcerers of Pharaoh's court, and yet he refused to free Israel. God sent plague after plague upon the land, but the hard-hearted king was unrelenting in his will to hold God's people in bondage.

In Exodus 12, God prepares and warns His people about the imminent destruction Egypt is about to experience and how they can protect themselves. How awesome that today, the Lord is again warning His children about the imminent destruction that is to come, but this time it will be in judgment of a pharaoh-like Antichrist who will someday soon hold humanity hostage.

The centerpiece of Exodus 12 is the spotless lamb. Also pictured here is Jesus giving His life for the freedom of all who will follow Him. God instructs the Israelites to apply the blood of the lamb to the sides and top of the doorposts of their homes (v. 7), and just as in our salvation, the blood is applied to the doorpost of our hearts. They were then instructed to eat the meat of the lamb (v. 8), symbolized in the New Testament by communion. They were told to eat in haste (v. 11), for Pharaoh, or in our case Satan, is perched, ready to destroy. In verse 12,

God declares that His judgment will be swift and awesome, as He brings punishment upon both man and beast. Many have questioned why the firstborn of the animals were slain here. It signifies God's disdain for the idolatry and worship the Egyptians displayed that centered on creatures. And then verse 13 powerfully instructs us about the blood of the lamb: *And the blood shall be to you for a token upon the houses where ye are: and when I see the blood, I will pass over you, and the plague shall not be upon you to destroy you, when I smite the land of Egypt.*

The blood is a sign of salvation, safety, and freedom for us today, as it was in the exodus. It is a sign for Satan too. It reads, "Hands off!" It says, "Devil, you cannot interfere or operate here – ever," for as verse 14 tells us, it is a lasting ordinance, one that must be spoken of and commemorated. Oh, how Satan surely does hate any talk of the blood, Beloved. Now look down at verse 22:

> *And ye shall take a bunch of hyssop, and dip it in the blood that is in the bason, and strike the lintel and the two side posts with the blood that is in the bason; and none of you shall go out at the door of his house until the morning.*

God instructed the Israelites to apply the blood of the lamb with the branch from a hyssop bush to the sides and top of the doorposts of their homes. This confirmed the protection of their going out and their coming in, their rest, their peace, their families, and their very lives. God also told them not to leave their homes until morning. To us, this symbolizes that to enjoy the blessings of His protection we must stay "in" Jesus – in close, abiding fellowship – until He calls us home to Him.

The hyssop bush is significant here. In King David's famous psalm of repentance, he cries out, *Purge me with hyssop, and I shall be clean: wash me, and I shall be whiter than snow* (Psalm

51:7). He's saying, "Oh God, I am sorry for my sins. Your grace and the mercy accompanying Your prescribed blood sacrifice is the only way out of my sinful state. Help me!" The hyssop was the carrier of the blood and its protecting and redeeming power. Though hyssop was pungent with mint fragrance, it held no healing nor saving powers within itself. However, the Israelites recognized that without it (or without some other heaven-chosen vehicle), the blood would lie unused in a time of great need, and the sacrifice of the lamb would have been for naught.

Just as we do not need to sacrifice another lamb, and just as we do not fight with physical weapons in our warfare, the carrier of the power of the blood is not an actual physical thing today. The blood was powerful to save Israel from the destruction of the "death angel," and played an instrumental part in bringing them their ultimate release from captivity in the exodus. In the same way, Christ's blood is powerful to save and bring us freedom from Satan's attacks today. But the blood required a carrier then, and it still does now. So what is the hyssop so sorely needed by God's people, the church? The answer is found in these verses from Romans chapter 10.

> *That if thou shalt confess with thy mouth the Lord Jesus, and shalt believe in thine heart that God hath raised him from the dead, thou shalt be saved. For with the heart man believeth unto righteousness; and with the mouth confession is made unto salvation.... For whosoever shall call upon the name of the Lord shall be saved.* – Romans 10:9-10, 13

Keeping in mind that without faith in your heart there is no freedom, the "hyssop" that brought the power of the blood in salvation for you is your tongue. The words *confess, confession,* and *call* all signify speaking to the Lord. Though God makes exception for any individual who has no physical ability to talk, for those of us who can, it is paramount to our salvation and for Christ's blood to cleanse our sins. Our obedience to speak in faith is the difference between being saved or lost. The very crux of salvation and of waging spiritual warfare is in our tongue.

Also, as we follow the word *hyssop* through the Scriptures, we cannot help but be struck by the fact that not only did God prescribe that branches of hyssop be the carrier for the blood of the protecting lamb in the exodus, but a hyssop branch was also used to lift up the sponge dipped in vinegar to Jesus' lips as He hung dying on the cross. We see this in John 19:29 and it is significant. Hyssop was integral in the freedom brought by the first Passover lamb. Here it plays a part again in the sacrifice of the second Passover Lamb. In John 19:30, Jesus uttered, *It is finished*, and then He died. We can rest assured that just three days later, Satan uttered, "I am finished." Praise God!

The Israelites were commanded to commemorate (to communicate about) the exodus with all future generations and to extol the power of God that delivered them from bondage. Today, the church must be reminded that success or failure for Christians is reliant on what we confess with our lips. Is it any wonder then that Satan wants our account of God's power and our witness for Christ to be silent and ineffective? He wants us to remain ignorant, insecure, and fearful of embarrassment, and by any means possible, to be kept in bondage. His goal for the Christian is to keep us from being the powerful soldiers God has called us to be. He will accomplish this if he can lessen or negate the importance of using the vehicle God prescribed for us to use in waging spiritual warfare.

Chapter 5

There's Power in the Word

And they overcame him by the blood of the Lamb,
and by the word of their testimony; and they loved
not their lives unto the death. – Revelation 12:11

We see here the Greek word *logos* translated "word" in the King James Version of the Bible. It simply means "to speak," or "something said," "utterance," "treatise," or "talk." The *logos* of God is His Word, the Bible, spoken to man. *Testimony* in this passage is *marturia* in Greek, or "something spoken," "evidence," "record of," "report," "witness," or "testimony."

This verse could read, "The saints of God defeated Satan by applying the power of the blood of Jesus Christ against his works. They spoke their report as witnesses for God of the evidence received and experienced through His salvation. These saints were so adamant in their battle against evil that their very lives did not count – only the victory in God!"

As we continue to examine this powerful passage, more truth flows out. First, the blood of the Lamb is a weapon we want to wield against the Enemy. Next, we see the key to using the weapon of the blood – the Christian testifying to the power of Christ's blood. Once we take a confident grip on what God has accomplished through the blood of the cross, the Enemy should take notice and flee. How can the Christian who understands his authority in Christ, his kingdom ambassadorship, and his awesome responsibility to herald this news ever be silent again? Our voice is the primary instrument to deliver the "payload" in spiritual warfare. Canadian author and evangelist Terry Law calls the lips the "launching pad" for the weapons of our warfare, which the Bible says are *mighty through God to the pulling down of strong holds* (2 Corinthians 10:4).

Though it sounds easy, a major obstacle awaits us. Many Christians are intimidated by the idea of waging spiritual warfare. Doing this is seen as radical, unsophisticated, spooky, or even scary. Fear of being thought of as weird for doing what the Bible says to do intimidates others. Some see it as somehow "charismatic." Regardless of what men say about the use of the tongue in spiritual warfare, we should follow God and see captives set free from the power of Satan. The gospel of Mark reflects Jesus' overriding concern with this very thing. In this gospel, we read repeatedly of Jesus' emphasis on deliverance from demons and disarming and binding the *strong man* (Mark 3:27). Jesus' numerous encounters with demons are all straightforward, head-on, with no avoiding the issue. Shouldn't it be that way for us, His disciples? How sad that so many wait and resort to doing what Scripture commands only when the chips are down, when Satan is winning, or when desperation sets in.

I Plead the Blood?

In times of spiritual warfare and travail, the old-time Baptists, Pentecostals, and others would declare, "I plead the blood." Though this saying may seem antiquated and foreign today, it was the standard among many who have effectively waged war against the Devil. What they were saying is, "I bring the power of the blood of Jesus to bear against the forces of evil." Or, "As God's ambassador, I apply the blood of Jesus, by faith, to any given situation, person, or thing." No matter what your doctrinal perspective may be, you cannot argue with the forthright tenacity of these saints who understood and fearlessly applied this principle.

The blood of Christ is an awesome, powerful, and protective covering, but is it everywhere? No. It must be applied by the saints of God. And just as the hyssop branch was used to apply the blood in the exodus, the blood does not accomplish what it can today without the proper paintbrush. We need to think of it like this: when the blood of the Lamb meets the word of our testimony, it's like nitro meeting glycerin. These entities depend on one another to create the intended effect. Both are powerful elements; however, individually they don't accomplish their mission, but together they are explosive!

Our Example is Jesus

Jesus taught by example, in love, in power, in healing, in justice. In fact, from the beginning of time, we can trace the paramount importance of the spoken word:

> God spoke the world into existence. The phrase *And God said* is found throughout Genesis chapter 1.

> Salvation comes by hearing the spoken Word of God (Romans 10:17) and then by speaking directly to God (Romans 10:9-10).

> Jesus spoke and Peter and Andrew followed Him (Matthew 4:19-20). Matthew did the same (Matthew 9:9), and Levi and Zacchaeus too (Luke 5:27-28; 19:1-9).

Jesus spoke and the storm ceased (Mark 4:39).

When Jesus fed five thousand people with two fishes and five loaves of bread (John 6:1-15), and four thousand people with seven loaves and a few small fish (Mark 8:1-9), He gave thanks. He spoke and there was more than enough to go around.

Jesus healed the sick and raised the dead by speaking to them (Mark 5:41-42; 7:31-37; Luke 5:12-15; 7:11-17; John 11:38-44).

Jesus dealt with demons by speaking to them (Mark 9:14-29; Luke 4:33-37).

And they came over unto the other side of the sea, into the country of the Gadarenes. And when he was come out of the ship, immediately there met him out of the tombs a man with an unclean spirit, Who had his dwelling among the tombs; and no man could bind him, no, not with chains: Because that he had been often bound with fetters and chains, and the chains had been plucked asunder by him, and the fetters broken in pieces: neither could any man tame him. And always, night and day, he was in the mountains, and in the tombs, crying, and cutting himself with stones. But when he saw Jesus afar off, he ran and worshipped him, And cried with a loud voice, and said, What have I to do with thee, Jesus, thou Son of the most high God? I adjure thee by God, that thou torment me not. For he said unto him, Come out of the man, thou unclean spirit. And he asked him, What is thy name? And he answered, saying, My name is Legion: for we are many. And he besought him much that he would not send them away out of the country. Now there was there

*nigh unto the mountains a great herd of swine feeding.
And all the devils besought him, saying, Send us into
the swine, that we may enter into them. And forth-
with Jesus gave them leave. [He spoke to them] And the
unclean spirits went out, and entered into the swine:
and the herd ran violently down a steep place into the
sea, (they were about two thousand;) and were choked
in the sea. And they that fed the swine fled, and told it
in the city, and in the country. And they went out to see
what it was that was done. And they come to Jesus, and
see him that was possessed with the devil, and had the
legion, sitting, and clothed, and in his right mind: and
they were afraid. And they that saw it told them how
it befell to him that was possessed with the devil, and
also concerning the swine. And they began to pray him
to depart out of their coasts. And when he was come
into the ship, he that had been possessed with the devil
prayed him that he might be with him. Howbeit Jesus
suffered him not, but saith unto him, Go home to thy
friends, and* **tell them how great things the Lord hath
done for thee, and hath had compassion on thee**.
– Mark 5:1-19 (author's emphasis)

Jesus instructed the man to go and testify of his deliverance.
Sound familiar? Yes. We are to testify of our deliverance from
captivity as well. By doing so, we let every human and every
spirit know who we are and in whose power we operate.

Scripture tells us that Jesus came to destroy the works of
the Devil (1 John 3:8). We can rest assured that the spilling of
His precious blood was enough to do so. But as Jesus walked
here on the earth, what example did He leave us in dealing
with Satan's lies, threats, and deceptions? In Matthew chapter

4, Satan comes to Jesus to tempt Him, and we see how Jesus battled back and won.

Then was Jesus led up of the Spirit into the wilderness to be tempted of the devil. And when he had fasted forty days and forty nights, he was afterward an hungered. And when the tempter came to him, he said, If thou be the Son of God, command that these stones be made bread. But he answered and said, It is written, Man shall not live by bread alone, but by every word that proceedeth out of the mouth of God. Then the devil taketh him up into the holy city, and setteth him on a pinnacle of the temple, And saith unto him, If thou be the Son of God, cast thyself down: for it is written, He shall give his angels charge concerning thee: and in their hands they shall bear thee up, lest at any time thou dash thy foot against a stone. Jesus said unto him, It is written again, Thou shalt not tempt the Lord thy God. Again, the devil taketh him up into an exceeding high mountain, and showeth him all the kingdoms of the world, and the glory of them; And saith unto him, All these things will I give thee, if thou wilt fall down and worship me. Then saith Jesus unto him, Get thee hence, Satan: for it is written, Thou shalt worship the Lord thy God, and him only shalt thou serve. Then the devil leaveth him, and, behold, angels came and ministered unto him.
– Matthew 4:1-11

Jesus had just fasted, and though spiritually empowered, He was physically weak. From both Scripture and experience, we know that Satan often attacks in our times of weakness. But here we know that Jesus' great life-changing ministry was just ahead of Him. He was about to deliver the greatest message of all time – the Sermon on the Mount (Matthew 5-7). So the message for us is this: when we are experiencing an unusual amount of spiritual warfare and attack, something great may be just around the next corner.

How did Jesus resist the Evil One? He used the weapon of the written Word of God. And since its instruction to us (the canon of Scripture) is now complete, in our post-crucifixion, post-resurrection age, what weapons should we choose in our struggle against the Enemy? The one that eternally finished off the Devil – the blood of Christ, mixed with God's Word in Jesus' name. We must acclimate ourselves to follow the example that Jesus set. He used the power of the spoken Word – directly against Satan himself – just as we must also do. Concerning the application of our weapons of spiritual war, there could be no better example than this.

Chapter 6

Does Satan Know Your Thoughts?

I the LORD search the heart. – Jeremiah 17:10a

Though some Christian teachers allude to Satan having the ability to read minds, we find no clear scriptural principle to back up this idea. We believe this is a strategic point for us to understand about the Enemy. Notice that the above Scripture from Jeremiah 17 (and many others) does point exclusively to God Himself as possessing the ability to search the heart and examine the thoughts of man. We find no evidence that any other being, Satan included, has any such access. As Proverbs 24:12 teaches us, God is the One who knows the heart and thoughts of man. He is the One who renders unto each of us accordingly. Can the Devil do likewise?

> *If thou forbear to deliver them that are drawn unto death, and those that are ready to be slain; If thou sayest, Behold, we knew it not; doth not he that pondereth the heart consider it? and he that keepeth thy soul, doth not he know it? and shall not he render to every man according to his works? – Proverbs 24:11-12*

God's Word deplores and even mocks the whole idea of fore-knowledge through divination by humans in His constant condemnation of occult practices. (See Deuteronomy 18:9-12, for example.) Why should we believe then that Satan could do it? True, he lives in the spirit realm and does have access to understanding, some of which we do not totally comprehend yet. Still, his power is indeed narrow, his ability to predict is at best limited to guessing, and he is certainly not omniscient. Most importantly, God forbids us to dabble in Satan's roulette wheel of occult deceptions, and for good reason.

The Bible indicates that not only is mind reading unreliable, but many times the results are tragic as well. Perhaps most sobering is Revelation 21:8, which tells us that witches, psychics, diviners, and the like are destined to an eternity in the lake of fire unless they repent and come to Christ. The occult is serious business in God's sight and, sadly, it is robbing people of millions of dollars in the world today, besides stealing them blind spiritually. From the booths manned by New Agers at your local county fair to the Internet, and, of course, late-night television, knowing the future is big, BIG business today. But do they really know the future, let alone the present circumstances of those inquiring about love interests, money, or other important issues? (More on this later.)

Life experience makes an argument against the idea of demonic thought reading as well. Though her life was undoubtedly captivated by some of Satan's most potent demonic workers, now-deceased astrological guru Jeane Dixon's prophetic success rate was only about 50 percent. Considering how nebulous some of her predictions were, even this figure is a very questionable percentage. Though her psychic abilities brought her great fortune and notoriety and seemed stunning to the unredeemed world, her works were nothing more than demonic manipulation to those who know the Bible. Though she did correctly predict some things and also claimed to have predicted numerous other events, she fell far short. In the Old Testament, under Jewish law, if a prophet was incorrect even once, he or she was taken to the gates of the city and stoned to death. This illustrates God's disdain for those who claim to speak for Him yet speak from their flesh or by another spirit instead. Thankfully, in these New Testament times, God is completely forgiving of all who have dabbled in witchcraft and sorcery if they come to Jesus and ask His forgiveness, surrendering their lives to Him.

Chapter 7

Silence Means Defeat

For by thy words thou shalt be justified, and by thy words thou shalt be condemned. – Matthew 12:37

Death and life are in the power of the tongue: and they that love it shall eat the fruit thereof.
– Proverbs 18:21

The main way that Satan and his minions can tell if you know your authority as a believer in Christ is by what you speak or what you do. Your actions and your words are paramount to your victory in the spiritual struggle with the powers of darkness. Since Satan and his forces cannot read our minds, we must recognize the importance of our words and deeds and their effect on our victory or defeat. The powers of hell can only gain information about our beliefs in this way.

More importantly, the single manner in which demonic forces are aware of our authority and our personal knowledge of this authority is by our declaration of Christ Jesus and His extended ambassadorship through us. Yes, as awkward, as foreign, and as radical as it may seem, only one way exists for a Christian to ensure the complete disarming of demonic powers. Our responsibility is to let the powers of darkness in our vicinity know that they had better do as the song says, "Pick up their weapons and flee." Do we just automatically expect every demon in every setting to know who we are in Christ?

An interesting question: When a demon encounters a Christian, does it automatically know the person is a Christian? I believe the answer is no. Demons are not omniscient nor omnipotent to immediately know our past history or automatically see our heart condition. Not even Satan can do that, for he is a mere finite being as well. Only God Himself has that ability, and though Lucifer loves to try to deceive people into thinking he's on par with God, he falls far short.

To use terminology from the golf course, the Devil's abilities are much like a triple bogey when compared to God's being like a hole-in-one in knowledge and understanding. For better or for worse, the Enemy's only route to gain information about individuals is through the actions and conversation of the person – not through reading thoughts. Our words and deeds are his means to really understand how to best trip us up and take advantage of us. His legal right to carry on many activities in our lives and homes ends when he realizes that we are not ignorant of his devices (2 Corinthians 2:11). Thus, he silently concedes that his limited power is no match for the One who controls our lives (1 John 4:4b).

We don't want the importance we have placed on vocalizing during spiritual battles to be misunderstood or to reinforce any extreme or negative views. By referring to the use of our voices, we are not encouraging the error that some have fallen into, producing utter paranoia concerning our everyday conversations. While we certainly believe one's words should be tempered in purity and reflect the principles of Scripture, some people seem to spend each waking moment afraid for their lives should they accidentally utter a negative statement. It's like trying to avoid a snare of the Enemy on one hand and falling into a different trap on the other.

Others have misunderstood the confessions of their lips to be a sort of mantra, which supposedly guarantees them God's favor. While we are adamant about using our voices as tools of spiritual warfare, we are in no way encouraging vain confession – a set of words strung together that allegedly assure health, wealth, and prosperity merely because we say them. Truly, negative words can cause emotional harm, allow the Devil a foothold to operate, and often reflect an attitude of someone living well below the joy of the Lord. Conversely, ignoring outright facts in order to say only positive things is often just plain lying.

On another extreme related to this, some are afraid to pray aloud for fear that they'll give away some secret to the Devil. They believe our petitions to God, the cares and concerns we express for others, or even our very Christianity, are to be kept within us in an effort to trip up the Enemy. Often Christians do repeat negative thoughts and perhaps need to rein in their tongues. But believing this is all that's needed for true spiritual warfare is counter to the principles the Scriptures lay out, and walking in such paranoia is certainly bondage.

Some teach that we need to ride along, take no firm position, and just let Jesus do the "heavy hitting." While there is an element of truth in this, it is only part of the picture. Does Ephesians 6:12 say, "For Jesus wrestles not against flesh and blood for us"? No, it tells us that we are *not* to wrestle against flesh and blood, but we *are* to stand against the armies of evil in the spirit realm. And while it is true that the battle is indeed the Lord's (2 Chronicles 20:15), He has given us very specific directions as to what part we play in His army and in the arena of spiritual warfare.

Our success in spiritual warfare won't be through ignorance. It won't be through self-reliance or good wishes. Our motivation for concentrating on this is to encourage every reader to see that we are powerless in spiritual struggles unless we unleash the tongue. Most Christians seem to be in a place of silence today, and we'd love to move them out and on into victory. With careful, bold declaration of God's truth and the time-tested biblical principle of testifying to these precepts, Satan can be bound, cast out, and handed defeat after defeat.

Chapter 8

The Psychic Hotline Is Called "Hot" for a Reason

And have no fellowship with the unfruitful works of darkness, but rather reprove them. – Ephesians 5:11

During our many years of ministry concerning the occult and related issues, we have never ceased being amazed at how often those claiming to be Christians seem completely oblivious to the origin and demonic nature of spiritualism. In our book *Entertaining Spirits Unaware: The End-Time Occult Invasion*, we presented a strong biblical case that exposes the roots of fortune-telling and the other "Nine Forbidden Practices" of the occult. Space will not permit us to revisit all the Scriptures and facts that expose psychic powers, fortune-telling, and witchcraft as traps of the Devil. But we do want to address the newly acquired "respectability" the occult and its practitioners have garnered recently. Getting involved, even innocently, with the occult will quickly put us on the losing end of spiritual warfare.

After a daily deluge of occult-based entertainment, advertising the viability of the paranormal, is it any wonder that we have such mainstream acceptance of these satanic practices? However, just because there is a growing psychic frenzy around us, we must not be deterred from our responsibility to rebut the occult whenever possible. Christians need to take part in this important facet of spiritual warfare. Regardless of the apparent mass approval of spiritualism, Bible believers must remain vigilant as we speak up concerning the occult. And remember, we'll be most effective when we calmly and carefully offer facts and biblical insight, even in the face of the relentless public relations campaign, which is meant to desensitize an unwitting public concerning Satan's devices. At the same time, be mindful that anytime we step out to expose the darkness, we must also be led by the Holy Spirit, covered in prayer, and endeavoring to remain steadfast in other facets of spiritual warfare.

Who's That Talking?

In the 1990s, one could not watch television for long without noticing an array of programming that featured the latest recognized psychic, or advertisements for pay-per-call services offering tarot card or other forms of fortune-telling. John Edwards offered false hope through supposed communication from beyond the grave for an hour each day on the syndicated show *Crossing Over with John Edward*. The mainstream network ABC elevated the overt occultism of David Blaine apparently without considering the spiritual nature of his powers. And the *Animal Planet* cable network developed a weekly series featuring an alleged pet psychic who claimed to be able to tell what your dog or cat is thinking. Please spare us!

But whether for canines or us humans, the rise and visibility of those claiming to have access to the other side is certainly parallel with the end of days predicted by the only reliable source for spiritual advice – the Bible. How tragic that so many who say they serve Christ also seek advice from the Devil's own sources or have no problem with such activities.

Setting our angst aside, relative to how a professing Christian might defend being entertained or even enlightened by the latest media-made fortune-teller, the question remains, how do these occult "prophets" really operate? How can a psychic give correct readings about the present circumstances of strangers, let alone predict the future? The answers are threefold, but are nonetheless entwined.

First, the leading and influence of demonic spirits feed the seer's mind with information about the "mark" Satan has lured into their counsel. Images, names, and other data the psychic gives about past or present events or personal relationships from the victim's life are intended to convince him or her that the psychic does have supernatural powers. This information that "comes" to the psychic's mind, sometimes in intimate detail, is a very powerful tool that has led many psychic seekers to trust in the occult darkness. When you think about it, how they do it should shock no one. The Devil knows history. Satan keeps good records pertaining to everything from individual lives to world events, with one intention – to deceive the unwitting. Just as Christians are filled and led by the Holy Spirit of God, those without Christ are subject to the leading and eventual possession of demons. W. C. Fields wasn't the first to say, "There's a sucker born every minute." That's a line right from Satan's ugly repertoire.

Second, sometimes psychics rely on pure speculation, especially about future events. Based on history, human nature, and his ability to garner elite information that may tip him off to possible future events, Satan places what seems to be prophetic information into the minds of fortune-tellers for them to make good guesses. Usually, the predictions are very general, with little detail. But because of a mediocre success rate, and in order to keep up their image for the sake of income, these less-than-stellar occultists sometimes just guess correctly about the past or the present to hopefully make it appear that they know the future.

The third part is demonically inspired events. For example, if a person actually believes the predictions made while playing with the Ouija board, the demons may, to varying degrees, set about to make the predictions of the satanic game become a reality. The same is true of psychic and tarot readings and following an astrology chart. If we give Satan room to influence our lives, he will try to seal the deal by orchestrating an event or circumstance that coincides with an occult prognostication we may have received. This is nothing more than a blatant attempt to manipulate our minds and gain our confidence and trust.

To accomplish his desired control over us, the Devil will use virtually any item to which humans ascribe significance. Whether it be an implement from occult tradition or a foothold caused by human idolatry, Satan's plan is first deception and then control. Lest we think that Satan cannot accomplish his ends by using other people, occult items, or personal idolatry, we need to be mindful of his status as *the god of this world* (2 Corinthians 4:4). Make no mistake – he is able to manipulate nature and circumstances for his purposes. It is right in Satan's wheelhouse to orchestrate the actions of demonically possessed people to make it appear as if the person on the other end of the telephone at the psychic hotline really did predict the future correctly.

If we begin exploring his camp to find answers to questions or solutions to our problems, we are in dangerous and forbidden territory. Can we expect God to automatically nullify the effects of any willful disobedience on our part? The answer is a resounding "No!" God warns us repeatedly to reject and flee from the world of darkness, yet we turn to everything from astrology to Zen, seeking answers and peace. This kind of occult manipulation, which has incredible and sometimes monumentally negative results for those who trust in it, is rife with horrific consequences.

As in Daniel's time, the Devil's crowd continues today. Occultists, purporting to know the future fortune or present trials of others, rattle off very impressive prophetic words that carry dramatic influence with those who have opened themselves up to demonic insight. These events sometimes represent very real spiritual experiences, and often fall on ears ready and willing to accept anything that comes along alleging to have the power to mend broken lives or fill a spiritual void. In fact, the modern New Age and occult movements have exploded because of the natural spiritual yearning within so many hearts that long to have one thing – verifiable spiritual experiences.

The sad fact is that countless millions desire spiritual enlightenment but remain resistant to the power of God. Many people continue to spend time, effort, and money chasing answers from sources that have already proven not to be trustworthy a great deal of the time. But for countless millions, the demonic bridge has been built, and the compulsion to enter Satan's forbidden sector of the spirit world seems overwhelming and nearly impossible to overcome. But praise God, Jesus did come to disarm the powers of darkness and bind the strong man (1 John 3:8; Matthew 12:28-29). And now we, His followers, have been given the grand task to infiltrate Enemy lines and implement His purpose and will. Amen!

Hooked on the Supernatural

All around us, people have developed a huge dependency on the occult as a means to find direction and leading for their lives. The world of psychics has found mainstream favor in our day because so many famous people, primarily from Hollywood, have opened the door to the spirit realm for themselves and then promoted it to the world at large. The result is that at this very moment, more people are trusting in demonic power, without even realizing it, than ever before. Captives are truly all around us in bondage to fortune-telling and soothsaying, people whom we as believers should view as a fertile field to reach and minister to in Jesus' name.

Countless thousands trusted in what the *Psychic Friends Network* told them (at $3.95 a minute) throughout most of the 1990s. Precious few gave it a thought when singer Dionne Warwick's occult phone service went bankrupt, though. It seems to us that if the "seers" employed there really knew the future, they would have seen the demise of the business coming. Yet, millions more are on Satan's waiting list, hankering to hear who they were in a past life or to find out what will happen next in this one.

Satan's Grand Counterfeit

All of this activity, whether packaged as New Age, psychic powers, astrology, numerology, or tarot cards, is but one thing – old-fashioned occultism. This is Satan's grand attempt to feign the Lord's supernatural works. The occult is Satan doing what he does best – counterfeiting God's actions and God's Word. Certainly, by knowing the history of his potential victims' lives (Satan surely does keep track), and by understanding human nature and human history, the Devil amazes the unsuspecting who walk into his territory looking for insight and direction. Most of his victims haven't a clue that once they cross the unseen barrier into his jurisdiction, they are actually fodder on the demonic playing field.

Satan's desired result of any such prophecy or information that humans receive via the occult is but one thing. The Devil wants people to believe that they can know the future, they can discover it, and they can manipulate powers in the spirit world. Actually, the opposite is taking place. *He* is in control and *they* are being manipulated. Satan then has his claws in them and continues to bait them until the lying spirits of confusion, fear, and even death work their trade to perfection.

Just as Paul warned the Ephesian church to not give the Devil a foothold (Ephesians 4:27), we remind our readers and audiences that no matter how enticing or innocent the psychic, New Age, or occult world may appear, it is strictly off limits for the believer. Moreover, our responsibility is to go beyond simple avoidance of the Enemy. Our obligation is to take him on (James 4:7; 1 Peter 5:8). He is the ultimate control freak, and we must oppose him actively and vehemently. If we accept this challenge, we're guaranteed one powerful outcome. When we walk in obedience to God's Word, captives are set free for the glory of God. And again, isn't that what it's all about?

Chapter 9

The Fascination with Fear

For God hath not given us the spirit of fear; but of power, and of love, and of a sound mind.
– 2 Timothy 1:7

Be strong and of a good courage; be not afraid, neither be thou dismayed: for the Lord thy God is with thee. – Joshua 1:9

Be strong and of a good courage, fear not, nor be afraid of them [pagan nations or practices]: for the Lord thy God, he it is that doth go with thee; he will not fail thee, nor forsake thee. – Deuteronomy 31:6

My people are destroyed for lack of knowledge: because thou hast rejected knowledge, I will also reject thee, that thou shalt be no priest to me: seeing thou hast forgotten the law of thy God, I will also forget thy children. – Hosea 4:6

As mentioned in the previous chapter, our book *Entertaining Spirits Unaware: The End-Time Occult Invasion* examined the "Nine Forbidden Practices" of the occult, which are listed in Deuteronomy 18:9-12. New Age occultism, witchcraft, and satanism depend on nothing more than a second-rate counterfeit of the truth of God's Word. They are a key part in Satan's warfare against us.

Experience dictates that once we understand the basis for these veiled and mysterious belief systems, the uneasiness, paranoia, and fear generated around them dissipates. The light of truth overpowers the darkness – information over ignorance. We are then able to go about our business of carrying on powerful, effective warfare in the spirit realm and more confidently act, witness, and minister in the natural realm.

In considering the subject of fear again, we must recognize how it is used as a tool to deceive and destroy many lives in our culture. Two aspects to this emerge. First, countless millions are prey for Satan as he injects fright, paranoia, and phobias into their lives. Second, millions around us undoubtedly love being frightened; Americans and Canadians spend hundreds of millions of dollars each year being entertained with themes rife with terror, death, and unhealthy suspense. We seem to know no limits in craving the rush of adrenaline associated with being scared and willingly pay those who produce it.

A lackadaisical attitude about violence and occult-based supernaturalism persists in our world that is unparalleled since the Dark Ages. Things that would have given our forefathers outright heart attacks have now become normalized. Not only have we become calloused and desensitized about death and respect for human life, but also our appetites for being fearfully entertained have drawn us to it, as if Satan himself has convinced us to love fear. He has followed this with a general fixation on the paranormal that is setting the stage for the masses to accept and crave every supernatural act the Antichrist will soon perform.

When Evil Becomes Good

Having a healthy fear, or reverence, for God is good, while fearing Satan is faithless and plays right into his hands. In our culture today, we see the general pronouncement that just about every theme mankind has historically shunned is now accepted. We have fallen into the snare of fear, which the Evil One has baited, promoted, and set with cunning accuracy. How strange that creatures created by God in His own image could be so ready and willing to walk into the perverted trap of adoring fear. Fear defeats us and disables the purposes of God in our lives. Fear is the antithesis of faith, so it's understandable that the Devil would want humanity to crave being frightened of what he has inspired. Using literature, folklore, superstition, and now the modern electronic media, Satan has used fear associated with the supernatural and the occult to infiltrate and captivate millions worldwide.

The Emotion of Fear

Do you realize that fear was the first emotion that Satan used in the heart of man to turn him away from God? Adam was in the garden, heard God's voice, and was afraid (Genesis 3:10). Fear is a tremendous emotion. Fear causes people to act irrationally, while a proclivity to or a craving for fear opposes the very basis of Scripture. Many Christians may bristle at this statement because they have developed an appetite for science fiction and horror novels, television, and motion pictures. Still, we question how a knowledgeable Bible believer could miss this. If you have a penchant for the macabre, we suggest a thorough reading of the latter part of 2 Corinthians 6, followed by a time of soul searching and prayerful repentance.

> *Be ye not unequally yoked together with unbeliev-*
> *ers: for what fellowship hath righteousness with*

*unrighteousness? and what communion hath light
with darkness? And what concord hath Christ with
Belial? or what part hath he that believeth with an
infidel? And what agreement hath the temple of God
with idols? for ye are the temple of the living God; as
God hath said, I will dwell in them, and walk in them;
and I will be their God, and they shall be my people.
Wherefore come out from among them, and be ye separate, saith the Lord, and touch not the unclean thing;
and I will receive you, And will be a Father unto you,
and ye shall be my sons and daughters, saith the Lord
Almighty.* – 2 Corinthians 6:14-18

The Progression of Fear

Fear has escalating properties built into it. As our culture
becomes more desensitized by and about fear, evil, horror,
the supernatural, pornography, death, and the lack of respect
for human life, we watch in dismay as the people of the world
grow increasingly violent. Unrest will continue to rise, and the
underlying tone will be an elusive quest for satisfaction of these
unholy and unhealthy desires that Satan has promoted. Surely
this will be one of the "fixes" that Antichrist will offer to the
craving but unsuspecting masses. A mass desensitization is
occurring as the spirit of fear becomes commonplace to even
the youngest of children. When they are filled with fear at an
early age, kids need more stimulation to get their adrenaline
pumping as they become accustomed to fear.

When we were kids, we watched *The Werewolf* and
Frankenstein. The werewolf was nothing more than a man
with a beard wearing a stocking cap over his head. That was
the werewolf; and in the 1950s, we were afraid. Now, children
seem emotionally and spiritually anesthetized concerning fear.

Today, fear has a dramatically different element than years ago, because fear is now created almost exclusively through themes based in the supernatural. For example, take the character Freddy Krueger from the now-aging movie series *Nightmare on Elm Street*. You don't just kill Freddy Krueger, because he comes back again and again. Therefore, no matter what the outcome of the movie or TV show, the thought projected is that Freddy lives on. Young people snicker at what once made us fearful. When we were young, very few realized that a progression of evil and an addiction to fear was about to sweep the world. Fewer still could have predicted the magnitude to which this addiction would negatively affect society – including the church.

Getting 'Em Young

Children today are getting heavy doses of fear, perhaps more than any generation before. In regard to general survival, previous generations have experienced harder and more treacherous day-to-day lives than we do. Our modern age and its advances in technology, medicine, communication, and transportation alleviate many life-threatening problems that were everyday disasters in the past. But in our culture, the past three to four generations have developed deep ties and addictions to the feelings associated with fear. Fear makes money and gets attention, and thus people decide to be scared – and scared good! Now it takes more and more fear to get high.

And because kids and their parents are making the choice to participate as recipients of fear, something else is happening. Kids today are getting involved in occultism, witchcraft, and demonism at an astounding rate. The incidence is higher than ever before. Why? Because that is the ultimate fear trip. Through a constant and favorable bombardment of supernaturalism over the past few decades, many teens and young adults have become desensitized to occult supernatural activities.

For entire generations, the occult has been favorably presented in many different forms since childhood. Though thankfully, not everyone who develops an affinity toward the paranormal delves heavily into it, the numbers of those claiming the occult as their belief system are very troubling. To many, it now seems normal to move from being a mere vicarious viewer to an active participant. This activity produced kids like Eric Harris and Dylan Klebold, whose satanic nightmare ended in a blaze of gunfire at Columbine High School in Littleton, Colorado.

One of the exhilarations being experienced by those dabbling in the occult kingdom is a false invincibility. This skewed view of reality leaves victims depending on false assumptions. Instead of the real love, joy, and sense of completion that one feels when surrendered to Christ, tens of thousands today have the perverted hope of some resemblance of satanic power in death. This is a sure and solemn sign that Jesus must be coming very, very soon.

The Crash of Our Culture

The desensitization and even estrangement from reality that takes place from large doses of fear through the childhood and adolescent years is partially the reason our culture has degenerated to where it is today. Sadly, without a moral shake-up, we wonder just how cold and calculating we might become tomorrow. We wonder how many saints of God may be living below the spiritual poverty level because Satan has worked his ways in them in earlier times and replaced the joy of the Lord with another type of otherworldly fascination. It happened with Lot, a righteous man, at Sodom. It can happen and is happening with many of us today.

Remember what we said earlier concerning joy? If you were Satan, wouldn't you do everything possible to drain the opposition of perhaps the most vital nutrient to the spiritual strength of the saints of God, replacing it with a counterfeit? We know that most people wouldn't equate their addiction to fear, sci-fi, or horror as a joy, but it either has replaced real joy or serves as a substitute in many lives. A person possessing the joy of the Lord is usually going to be a dangerous witnessing instrument against the Devil. However, can you imagine a Christian feeling driven to tell someone about the love of Jesus after watching any of the horrific programs or movies that are out today? Think back to the last time that you watched a TV show or movie that capitalized on violence, horror, or the occult. Imagine how you felt afterward and now ask yourself these questions:

- Did I feel like studying the Bible?

- Did I feel like worshiping the Lord?

- Did I want to go and witness for Jesus?

If you answered "no" to these questions, you can see how Satan is stifling many of God's people and bringing division into Christian homes through fear addictions today.

How wonderful to know that the power and blood of Jesus can deliver people from all their unsavory activities and free them from the mistakes of the past. But this often comes with a struggle. Sometimes the scars run deep from a childhood of fear-induced conditioning, whether from television, movies, or real-life circumstances and events. Be assured, the church is not immune to this phenomenon of fear and its side effects.

Occult Fear and Generational Spirits

Several years ago in western Canada, I (Eric) was present-ing my *Take A Stand!* seminar series in a local church. At the close of the evening and after the invitation for those needing to come forward for prayer, I had the opportunity to pray and counsel with a young church member who was about twenty years old. This young lady, professing to be a Christian, had become addicted to violence and fright. She craved it, desired it, and like any addiction, had to have it – right or wrong. She told me, "I know it's wrong, but I love being scared and I want God to take it away from me."

I assured her that God did not want her frightened or drawn to fear. This girl's problem had escalated to the point that when she attempted to read the Bible, she only wanted to read Old Testament passages that described war and death. For several minutes, we knelt at the altar of that little church and, as I prayed, God began to move. Leading her in a prayer of repentance, but still sensing that there was more to be dealt with, I asked her if she had ever been involved with the occult, either casually or avidly.

The girl began to sob uncontrollably as she described her family's involvement in occult séances. During these séances years earlier, she had witnessed objects levitating, among other occult practices. Though she indicated that she had not been an active participant, she did recount how she would cower in a corner from fear during these séances. Armed with this insight, I led her to renounce all ties with the occult. After a few minutes of prayer, I sensed that God was finished, at least for the time being.

The next night the girl came to the seminar, sat in the front row, and came to me afterward exclaiming, "Wow! Last night I read the book of Psalms for the first time!" She indicated that since the night before, she had experienced no desire to continue the practice that had bound her for so long. Praise the Lord! She wrote a few weeks later and reported that she was continuing in her newfound freedom in Jesus.

I wrote back and rejoiced with her, but added a warning. She was on her way to being free, but there was still work to do. Often saints declare victory in the war after the first battle.

We know that Satan does not give up easily, and he may come back, accusing, reminding us of the past, and trying to lure us back into it. However, I counseled her that if she is persistent in her faith and diligent in her walk with God, she can overcome. What victory we have in Jesus' name! What it takes is an unyielding attitude of surrender.

This young lady's entrapment by satanic forces came from the fear she experienced by merely being subjected to witnessing occult séances – not from participation. Though only a viewer, as she grew older, her life reflected the fear Satan's forces had planted in her years before. The church today seems to struggle with the idea that although someone has received Christ and has lived as a Christian, they are not free in this area. Does this reflect a weakness in Christ's power to deliver? Of course not. An inventory of our lives as believers would most likely indicate how we have grown in Him and progressed in freedom. This girl simply had not dealt with nor realized the need to deal with the root cause of her fear before that night in church.

The possibility also exists that her family's ties to the occult may have increased the potential of her being bound by the Enemy as well. Scripture and experience teach us that the sins of our fathers can and frequently do visit themselves upon future generations (Exodus 20:5; 34:7; Numbers 14:18; Deuteronomy 5:9), even if the latter may have had no physical contact whatsoever with the former. Though we often want something from God in our own timing, He knows our needs but may have other plans for His purposes to come to fruition in us.

God has a marvelous way of positioning us in the right place and at the right time to deal with issues in our lives. The key to this is our willingness to do what He has directed, when He directs. But we must be able to hear what He is directing us to do in the first place, which is dependent on having fellowship with Him daily. The key to victory is always being humble, teachable, and ready to submit to the Lord when He shows us how to deal with areas of trial and struggle. Otherwise, we'll deepen the hole that the Devil wishes us to dig for ourselves and delay or even destroy the progressive deliverance God has planned for us.

Your Freedom May Be a Choice

Some who read this book have been oppressed by spirits that gained a foothold through incidental or purposeful occult involvement. However, many more may have opened the doors of hell because they allowed a habit of amusement through science fiction and horror to wrap its way around their hearts. Many times churchgoers have vehemently disagreed with us on this issue, but the fact remains that one of Satan's life-choking gateways into Christian lives has been through the *angel of light* of ungodly, dark entertainment. If we expect to walk in victory, we must be aware that Satan takes these aspects of spiritual warfare seriously. In *Entertaining Spirits Unaware*, we examined some "Doorways to the Devil" that Christians are either indifferent to or purposely choose to be ignorant of. One thing we can be assured of is this: we are destined to lose in spiritual warfare unless we take inventory of and deal with the seemingly harmless things we have allowed to infiltrate our lives and homes. How can we expect God to bless us, our homes, and our families if we insist on being entertained by books, movies, and music, which are working in concert directly against the written Word and will of God?

We cannot afford to discount the Enemy's willingness to drag us into his clutches in whatever way he can. And though we may name Jesus as our Savior, Satan's destructive desire is to operate through the access to our lives he may have enjoyed before we met Christ. Remember that the story above is one of a Canadian teenager who claimed to be a born-again believer in Christ who was a victim of satanic power dating back to her childhood. There is a message here.

Regardless of how long the process may be or how many steps it may take, Jesus came to deliver us completely! Once more, we ring the alert bell of Hosea 4:6 that God's people are indeed *destroyed for lack of knowledge*. The Greek word translated *salvation* exclusively in the New Testament is *soteria* (so-tay-ree´-ah). *Strong's Exhaustive Concordance of the Bible* translates this word as "deliver," "health," "salvation," "save," and "saving." Truly, salvation is a work of deliverance, giving health (spiritual, emotional, mental, and physical) and the once-granted and ongoing act of redemption.

Perhaps you've heard the statement, "I was saved, I am being saved, I will be saved." How true this is as we walk, learn, and trust deeper each day in God's love and protection. The same is true of our deliverance as well, which is a process as we gain more freedom from the forces and intrusion of evil. Scripture could accurately read, "For whosoever shall call upon the name of the Lord shall be **delivered**" (Romans 10:13, author's emphasis and paraphrase).

Our salvation, redemption, healing, and deliverance are truly a process. But we must cooperate with the Lord if we are to realize our ultimate freedom in Him. Through a lack of understanding or a willful choice of disobedience, we can interfere with the fullness and completion of what God intends for His children here on earth. We are not inferring that, just because there is evidence of Satan attempting to intrude or actually doing so in an individual's life, this is always a sign of demon possession, or that in the case of a Christian, his or her eternal salvation itself may be in jeopardy. Satanic attacks on our lives are not a sign of God's rejection or disapproval of us, nor are they necessarily evidence that there is sin present. Satanic attacks are usually just part of the territory of living as a Christian. But resisting God's desire to see us set free is to work in opposition to the Holy Spirit. The lies of the Enemy tell us that either we can enjoy any vicarious pleasures without consequence, or we can never be free, so why bother trying.

I (David) remember an occasion while ministering in a church when yet another teenage girl, bound by the Devil, approached the altar.

Shaking, she said, "Mr. Benoit, I can't be saved."

I answered, "What do you mean, you can't be saved?"

She said, "I can't be saved."

She started to slowly pull up her long, black dress. As she inched her dress up, she revealed a demonic symbol of a dragon tattooed on her calf.

She said, "Mr. Benoit, that's my pact with the Devil, and I can't get my soul back. He's got my soul."

Wrong! At that very instant, he did not own her soul any more or less, just because she may have made some sort of pact with him. Over the course of the next few moments, I ministered the truth from God's Word to her, which culminated in the girl's praying to receive Jesus as her Savior. No "pact with Satan" or demonic tattoo can stop the love and power of God! Amen.

Who Owns You?

We often run across people who believe that they can never be free because of some past event or experience in their life. This is a common scenario and is nothing short of the intimidation of Satan. Look at it logically. Before a person is saved, the Devil already has their soul. Jesus made that clear when he stated that a person who was not with Him was against Him (Matthew 12:30; Luke 11:23). In these words, Jesus crushed the notion that a person could ride the fence about commitment to Him and opposition to evil. His condemnation of attempted neutrality leaps off the pages of Scripture, through time, to us today.

In a world so confused by compromise, His words are crystal clear. Like it or not, know it or not, a person walking without Christ is walking with the Devil – no matter how good or righteous he thinks he might be. So it is with the case in point. You cannot barter with that which you do not own. If the Devil already has your soul, he's not going to barter with it. Satan never educates his victims to understand that before they got involved in witchcraft or satanism, they were already his. He just intimidates people to believe that once they make a pact with him, they are then doomed to fulfill their obligation. This lie is a great tool with which to bind people. Likewise, teaching people that once they make a pact with the Devil their soul can never be redeemed is dangerous and unbiblical. No power of hell exists that cannot be broken by the power of Jesus Christ. None.

Jesus can, will, and does set any captive free who calls on Him. The Devil cannot own someone who comes to Christ and invites Him into his or her life by faith. Nor can he ever withhold salvation and deliverance from anyone who calls on the Lord and asks.

Walking in His Lordship

To the believer in Christ, freedom from fear, especially from habits that make us fearful, is an issue of lordship, living in the victory God intended for us to experience. In the great spiritual warfare passage we paraphrased from above (Matthew 12:25-37), Jesus made no room for His followers to volitionally pick and choose which evil practices or vices they would stand against. This moves in concert with another interesting fact. The New Testament equates Jesus as Savior only sixteen times, but it refers to Him as Lord on more than four hundred and fifty occasions. Yet countless Christians continue to attempt to separate His salvation/deliverance from His lordship in their lives.

Though inconsistent with what the apostles taught, many hold this view today – the majority of whom have probably never thought it through. If the full measure of His salvation can be attained without the effort and willingness of our surrender, how can we call Him Lord? If the issue of salvation is all that Christianity is about, then we could try to hang on to many ideals, habits, and practices that His lordship beckons us to cast aside. The real issue then is how we decide to live and how much of ourselves we are willing to give. Can we expect the full measure of His blessings, protection, and promises to be active in our lives if we resist His call of lordship?

We need to ask ourselves this question: whether there be just a day or several decades left in our life here on earth, why would we ever want to stand in the way of God's perfect will, richest blessings, and complete work in our life? The answer lies only in original sin – we want things our way. The remedy lies only in complete surrender to Him.

Chapter 10

Examining the Armor of God

Truth and Righteousness

No army has ever been victorious that did not know its enemy. General Norman Schwarzkopf commanded the assault known as Operation Desert Storm, which liberated the country of Kuwait from Saddam Hussein's invading Iraqi troops in 1991. Could you imagine Schwarzkopf addressing his troops by saying, "Listen. I can't stand Saddam Hussein; never have liked the man. So, I don't want to talk about Saddam Hussein today. I've just come to praise President George Bush. No need to discuss our enemies; let's just say nice things about our friends."

Doesn't that sound stupid? More so, it would have been no way to prepare for battle. If General Schwarzkopf had exhibited a lack of quality leadership, we would have lost many lives and possibly met a resounding defeat in the Gulf War. Instead, he laid out a finely tuned battle plan that was replete with intense reconnaissance. Schwarzkopf made certain to give his troops a correct understanding of who the enemy was, their abilities, weaknesses, strengths, tactics, habits, and where they would most likely operate and with which weapons. Our men knew how to fight that war because of their training, their understanding, their willingness to follow the specific orders given by their commander, and their knowledge of the enemy.

Comforting the Enemy – Discord, Lies, the Flesh

The Bible contains much information to help us defeat the Enemy, but we must *know* the Book – not just say that we believe what it says. Ignorance in spiritual matters is akin to ignorance in court. You may be innocent and you may be well intentioned, but ignorance may cost you dearly. We can repeatedly say that we trust the Bible as God's written Word and sole authority for mankind, but if we haven't explored it to know exactly what God proclaims, our words are empty statements.

How can we ever be the overcomers, bold and powerful, that God would have us aspire to be without knowing His will and our authority as given by Him? So, let's go on a little "recon" mission to examine the operation of our Enemy while we train ourselves to be obedient to our Commander. When it comes to victorious Christian living, Ephesians chapter 6 is the best place to start.

> *Finally, my brethren, be strong in the Lord, and in the power of his might. Put on the whole armour of God, that ye may be able to stand against the wiles of the devil. For we wrestle not against flesh and blood, but against principalities, against powers, against the rulers of the darkness of this world, against spiritual wickedness in high places. Wherefore take unto you the whole armour of God, that ye may be able to withstand in the evil day, and having done all, to stand. Stand therefore, having*

your loins girt about with truth, and having on the breastplate of righteousness; And your feet shod with the preparation of the gospel of peace; Above all, taking the shield of faith, wherewith ye shall be able to quench all the fiery darts of the wicked. And take the helmet of salvation, and the sword of the Spirit, which is the word of God: Praying always with all prayer and supplication in the Spirit, and watching thereunto with all perseverance and supplication for all saints. – Ephesians 6:10-18

Are we living in the prophetic last days, which Scripture teaches become progressively more evil? Absolutely (Matthew 24). Do we have a cunning opponent who wishes to devour us? Absolutely (1 Peter 5:8). And, do we not have a powerful Lord who shed His own blood to give us the victory in these darkened end times? Absolutely. Praise the Lord! So then, victory seems contingent on our being faithful, with time spent in study, in prayer, and in obedience.

The Bible says *we wrestle not against flesh and blood*, but rather with spiritual powers that surround us (Ephesians 6:12). We must specify that our war is ultimately against evil spiritual beings. We often struggle with human forces as we contend to establish righteous viewpoints. However, whether through dialogue, debate, exposé, or other means, the bottom line must remain crystal clear – humans are not the enemy of the believer.

The cornerstone of Christianity is John 3:16, which teaches that God so loved the world that He sent His only Son. We need to remember that if it wasn't for His mercy and grace, it could be (and maybe once was) us campaigning for abortion, globalism, or so many other causes inspired by the Devil. Let's never forget that unregenerate flesh has a habit of falling in with Satan's wishes. The unredeemed may speak for the Devil unabashedly and unknowingly, but they should not be seen as the Devil. Often in the midst of confrontation, we lose sight of who the real Enemy is and begin to see other humans as our foe. The manipulations of the powers of hell only make it seem as though people are the enemy.

However, that's no signal for the redeemed to think they are immune from Satan's plan and attacks. Satan can attack us too, and his plan may often masquerade in the name of something sounding quite noble – yet quite unbiblical. The Devil wants to deter us from fulfilling God's wishes and plan at all costs. He'll enter through any open door we grant him and he is constantly looking to exploit our weaknesses and gain the upper hand.

The demonic forces Paul refers to in Ephesians 6 and elsewhere in Scripture make a practice of interfering in our daily lives and can hinder every part of our existence, if we allow them. If we're not vigilant to follow the Scriptures and stand for righteousness, the Devil may gain a free rein. Our churches are replete with born-again folks who will attest to what we are saying. These Christians have experienced firsthand the relentless attacks of Satan on their lives, and, having allowed their spiritual lives to fall into disrepair, have unwittingly given Satan access, sometimes with tragic consequences. A featured practice of Satan's workers is to sow discord and lies and to convince us to operate merely from our flesh in spiritual matters.

To elaborate: Some who are reading this book are constantly at odds with a coworker; you rationalize that you just have a personality conflict and just can't like everybody. Certainly, in offices, factories, and businesses today, there is no shortage of the attitudes and junk seen on soap operas and *The Jerry Springer Show*. Have you ever thought that the problems in some of our relationships could be partially a product of demonic meddling? Perhaps due to a lack of knowledge and a proper view of spiritual warfare, many of us are simply unequipped to recognize and deal with it as such.

So, regardless of how uncomfortable – even maddening – some relationships may be, shouldn't we always be praying and asking God to guide us and bring change for His glory? After all, doesn't His Word promise that He is working out everything for His purpose and for our good (Romans 8:28)? Often, dedicated Christians find themselves enslaved to bitterness, or even hatred, as we think it better to just despise someone's actions and be at odds with them. When this happens, the spiritual war is being waged to determine how we will act and react as we walk through this life.

We often refer to "Spirit-filled living" as we discuss our walk with the Lord. Have you stopped to think that if we aren't filled with the Holy Spirit, we might be influenced by another spirit? No, this is not necessarily referring to demon possession, but rather demonic manipulation – one of the Devil's key tools promulgating discord, lies, and fleshly desires. When you are tempted to hate someone (or commit any other act of disobedience to God), pause, pray, and ask God to help you see them through His eyes before you allow your fleshly attitude to act in its fallen state. Whether it's through a chink in your armor or by means of subtle intrusion of demons into your mind and will, Satan's purposes are realized if you react otherwise.

I (David) have a pastor friend who told us that every morning he and his wife pray together. It doesn't matter where they are. If one of them is out of town, they will call each other just to pray. He said they do this because it's hard to fight with your spouse at night when you know you're going to pray together in the morning. Could some of the arguments we have with our husband or wife be spiritually induced as well? Shouldn't we say, "Let's stop, honey. Let's pray about it." Sometimes it's easier to fight a little bit instead of coming before the Lord with our differences. It sounds foolish, but it's true.

Have you ever noticed that Sunday mornings are often the most tense time of the week? When we try to get ready for church, everything seems to happen. Besides the fact that we are fallible humans who let our flesh act and react, too many homes are in disarray on Sundays (Monday through Saturday too?) because we are in a spiritual war and haven't come to grips with it. Praying for the Lord's intervention in our struggles with one another is definitely an act of spiritual warfare and not one Satan wants us to commit.

Truth or Consequences?

Wherefore take unto you the whole armour of God,
that ye may be able to withstand in the evil day, and
having done all, to stand. Stand therefore, having
your loins girt about with truth.
– Ephesians 6:13-14a

If we are in a spiritual battle, we had better be armed with God's truth and be willing and ready to use it. God does provide perfect and impenetrable armor to protect us. We're going to need it. The first thing He tells us is that we ought to have our belt around us. From what we gather in history, men in ancient times did not dress for battle in pants such as we wear today. They would fight in long tunics, like long dresses. They would tie their belts to pull their hemlines up, so they wouldn't trip over them. Could you imagine being in the heat of battle and stepping on your hemline? In the same way, we must uphold truth, God's standard for trust, no matter how unpopular it may be with others or with our own flesh. Practicing lies, deception, and fabrication of facts is a surefire method to demolish our spiritual strength and allow Satan the right to tap-dance all over our lives.

The Bible says we should have our *loins girt about with truth.* Have you ever heard someone say, "He tripped over his own lie"? That came from this passage in Ephesians 6. Lying becomes habitual. For example, if you're going to lie to your wife, you had better have more than one lie ready, because it seems that most ladies don't ask questions in packs of ones or twos. They come in a series of inquiries that unravels until you are tripped up with no place to go. Chances are she already had it figured out, if you've fallen for Satan's plan and have begun to make a practice of sidestepping the truth in your daily life together.

Teenagers know all about this. If they walk by their dad and say, "See you later, Dad. I'm going to Johnny's house," most dads say, "See you later, son."

Most mothers, however, see through their children's deceptiveness. You walk by your mother and say, "See you later, Mom. I'm going to Johnny's house," and she says, "Hold on a minute. Who is this Johnny person? I've never met him. How old is he? Is he a Christian? What kind of family does he come from?" And finally, "Has he ever been to the penitentiary?" She's going to ask you thirty questions before you walk out the door.

We're sure not belittling anyone here. However, because of our fallen human nature, we have learned how to lie without lying. It's called the sin of distortion, and it's not really lying in the classical definition, but it's not really telling the truth either. Some men even claim this is a defense against their wives' use of the "gift of suspicion."

Often we find ourselves skirting the truth to keep from getting caught in something that others (our mates in particular) may not approve of or simply to get our way. Ninety-nine percent of the time, if this becomes a habit, a deeper root problem exists in the relationship that needs to be addressed. Regardless, hedging on the facts, or skirting issues to manipulate a situation, is not telling the truth, is it? And God wants truth. Skating around the edges is essentially saying that God couldn't give us His divine favor in any given situation by being forthright and honest. Granted, some things are better left unspoken, but an honest answer will always strike against the powers of darkness.

Now listen to this carefully. This does not mean we need to be brutal with the truth in order to please God. Our interactions should have the element of grace and love intertwined in them, even in times of rebuke or correction or when anger arises. Being truthful in touchy situations is an art that only the Holy Spirit and our mindset of obedience to Him can corporately execute for God's glory.

We have told our kids (and grandchildren) that God wants us to be truthful, even when it hurts and puts us in a position we may not like. Chances are if we feel the desire to fib in a situation, it's because we have positioned ourselves by some other act that's unbecoming to the kingdom of God. But more so, we find ourselves in that situation because we have determined that lying has the possibility of getting us what we want, and we have chosen to ignore being truthful when it's to our advantage.

This is a mindset induced purely by satanic leading, which is rooted in rebellion. When we yield to the temptation to lie, it slowly becomes a lifestyle – a habit and a constant sin. God surely abhors lies, as Revelation 19 tells us. He most certainly wants His children to seek the truth, live the truth, and speak the truth as a lifestyle choice, for it is certain that lying opens our lives up to the work of the Devil and weakens our position as victors in Christ.

More Thoughts on What Constitutes a Lie

For out of the abundance of the heart the mouth

speaketh. A good man out of the good treasure of the
heart bringeth forth good things: and an evil man
out of the evil treasure bringeth forth evil things. But
I say unto you, That every idle word that men shall
speak, they shall give account thereof in the day of
judgment. – Matthew 12:34b-36

Please understand that we don't claim to have every answer on this issue. We want to provoke you to examine the words you say, for they have paramount importance in the outcome of your spiritual battles. In the passage above, Jesus was mincing no words concerning how God views the heart and words of evil men. If it is so for the unredeemed, how much more does God expect His own children to walk and speak uprightly? But let's interject a big dose of God's grace right here, for we are not writing this to lay guilt trips or legalism on anyone. However, we do want everyone to look at their lives and relationships to evaluate if they measure up to God's standard.

Some situations are difficult to walk through, so the intentions of the heart may determine whether something could qualify as a lie or not. Thankfully, that's not our department, but God's.

Consider this example as food for thought along these lines. The story is told about a pastor in the middle of a revival. This dear little saint walked up to him and said, "Pastor, I want to give you and the evangelist a pie." He thanked her and took the pie home. After their first bite of the pie, both the pastor and the evangelist agreed that it was the worst-tasting pie they had ever had, and they threw it in the trash.

The next night at church, the dear old saint asked the pastor what they had thought of her pie. He stopped and thought, and then he said, "Ma'am, let me tell you something. Pie that tastes like that doesn't last long around our house."

Now, he didn't outright lie, but the manner of his inference did not reflect the entire truth either. How would you have handled this situation? Is there a single pat answer? Should he have said, "Well, we both agreed that your pie was the worst dessert served yesterday on the entire planet!" Probably not. He would have harmed her spirit and would have rejected her act of kindness. He also might have destroyed his relationship with her and could have caused her to walk away from church and never return.

Perhaps not addressing specifics or not saying too much was the best way to handle that situation so as not to hurt someone who was merely engaging in a well-intentioned act of kindheartedness. However, there is a marked difference between trying not to crush the spirit of a kindhearted soul and saying things laced with half-truths for personal gain. This is the core of the issue.

My (David) adoptive father is a gourmet cook. This man can cook anything, but his mother couldn't cook a lick. So when he eats at someone's house and he doesn't like the way they have prepared the food, he says, "That's just like what Mama used to make." We hope you see what we are getting at here. People learn how to be deceptive without thinking it's really lying. But God's standard is that His children ought to be forthright. Not that we always need to be so blunt that we're mean, but above everything, shouldn't we use truth in our tact? The Bible says we need to put the rope of truth on our loins and somehow, if we are willing, God will give us the ability to be truthful; we just need to trust Him. The cornerstone of truth is yieldedness to God.

Righteousness

And having on the breastplate of righteousness.
– Ephesians 6:14b

In ancient times, the breastplate was very important to a warrior because it would have been nearly suicidal to go into battle without it. These people were shooting arrows; they were throwing spears; and they were fighting with swords. If you didn't have your heart and your lungs covered, you'd have been an open target for them.

The Bible instructs us to operate covered by the breastplate of righteousness. Do you know what righteousness is? The Greek word translated *righteousness* in Ephesians 6:14 is *dikastes*, which, simply put, means "just judgment." *Webster's New Collegiate Dictionary* defines righteousness as "acting in accord with divine or moral law; free from guilt or sin; morally right or justifiable." In short, righteousness is "right living." It's training to do the right thing, which is not the natural thing to do, but is contrary to our fallen nature and denotes our separation from it.

Righteousness is a heart attitude that becomes our way of life through obedience to the Lord and surrender to His will. Right living is a decision, but we see that in the end it emanates from our yieldedness to God. His righteousness is what makes us able to walk against the desires of our human flesh, which is a constant venue for spiritual warfare. God's supernatural righteousness gives us the ability to overcome the temptations to do the wrong thing. Jesus went to the cross, in part, so we could have "right living." Do we really trust what He gave us if we manipulate people and situations through the less than truthful use of our tongue? Deception is certainly not acting in accordance with what the "Just Judge" freed us to be.

Chapter 11

Shoes and a Hat to Match

And your feet shod with the preparation of the gospel of peace. – Ephesians 6:15

S hoes in ancient times were very important. They were so important that they were the only piece of clothing the children of Israel wore continuously for forty years. Not a red pair for Tuesday and a blue pair for Thursday, but one pair of shoes for forty years. One reason these shoes were so important was that the Israelites fought their battles in the hot sand.

We both grew up near water and sandy beaches. I (David) grew up in Louisiana, not too far from the beaches of the Gulf of Mexico, and Eric grew up in a town in West Virginia, situated right on the Ohio River. Like most kids going to the beach, we learned firsthand that even though there is cool water nearby, the sand is unusually hot. The point is that we can't fight a battle when our feet are on fire. We can try to run, but all we really do is concentrate on how uncomfortable our feet are.

A person can't win spiritual battles without having solid footing either. The shoes of the gospel of peace are not just about our winning a battle and walking in salvation ourselves. Others are depending on us (though they may not know it) to share the truth of God's salvation message with them. The good news is that God has given us long-lasting, protective, and anointed footwear for our journey here on earth.

These shoes in Ephesians 6:15 are the finest designer model available. They are constructed for battlefield use, to protect and serve the wearer in adverse situations; and unlike the type we buy at the department store, they only get stronger with use. They were designed to assist us in spreading the gospel and enable us to defend the faith. They are not cheap shoes, but they are free to all who will pick up the cause and join the army. The price tag was more than we could ever afford ourselves, for these shoes were purchased with the earthly life and death of our Savior, Jesus Christ. Wear them with Him in mind and with His kingdom's business as their purpose. Walk in the power they represent, knowing these shoes are sealed in His blood. No matter how hot the sands of battle might be, they'll withstand it all.

Separately, we have had the opportunity to minister to and with many sports figures – the Boston Celtics, Philadelphia 76ers, Atlanta Hawks, Indianapolis Pacers, Washington Wizards, and other professional teams, as well as many on the PGA Tour. The list even includes sports figures such as baseball great Dave Dravecky. In every case, one thing is a constant – sports figures know their equipment, starting with their shoes.

In the case of the basketball teams, when these guys come in, some of them are seven feet tall, and we can assure you that these men don't have normal feet. We're not talking size twelve, thirteen, or fourteen; we're talking size eighteen, nineteen, and twenty. These shoes don't have those little pumps. You'd have to use an air compressor to put that much air in that much shoe. The point is that you will never see a professional basketball player come to a pre-game chapel service wearing baseball cleats. Nor will you see a professional baseball player come to a game with golf shoes on. They wear the shoes that are designed for their particular sport. And the shoes that we find mentioned in Ephesians 6 are designed to spread the gospel.

Likewise, the helmet of salvation is fit for its purpose. The most precious element in the protective or defensive suit of armor in biblical times was the helmet, because it often made the difference between life and death in the hand-to-hand combat of most battles. A person could receive many wounds and live, but a wound to the head would often spell death.

The same is true for us. The helmet is still a vital item in a soldier's outfit, and just as it is a lifesaver in times of war, our helmet of salvation is a lifesaver too – an eternal lifesaver. God's analogy of salvation being a helmet is no accident. The helmet symbolizes the protection of the most crucial things in our physical lives on earth – our minds, eyes, and ears; and it is related to the most crucial element in eternity – our salvation. *And take the helmet of salvation* (Ephesians 6:17a).

Our salvation is the part of our walk with God that we need to take complete grasp of. Countless Christians walk through their lives in abject fear about their place in eternity. How tragic. A person who is in constant fear of his place and acceptance with God will never be able to do the great things God has called him to do. He will be, however, exactly where Satan wants him – powerless, fearful, and usually silent.

A person should fear if he or she is living in sin, but in our combined thirty-five-plus years in ministry, we have seen that the church needs a good dose of who they really are in Christ. If we realize the awesome nature of what God has done for us and what He has commissioned us to do for Him, the effects upon the lost world and the kingdom of darkness would be staggering. Satan wants an anemic, confused church – one consumed with fear and filled with people who walk without the knowledge and assurance of their own salvation. This is not only the very heart of the issue of spiritual warfare for many, it is also the thread that sews the banner of evangelism as well.

Part of defending the faith (Jude 3) is being ready to give every man an answer for the hope that lies within us (1 Peter 3:15). Many Christians are lost for words when challenged about why they believe what they believe. Our lack of knowledge or inability to articulate our salvation to others causes us to retreat instead of going forward and taking back ground from the Enemy. We fail in perhaps the most eminent part of spiritual warfare simply because we are not prepared and studied in the very thing we contend is most important.

We need to examine ourselves right now. Do we know why we believe what we do about salvation, the authenticity of the Bible, or even Jesus and His death, blood, resurrection, and forgiveness? If not, we need to make it a point of ultimate importance and explore God's Word and other study helps for answers. We guarantee that when the Mormons or Jehovah's Witnesses come to our doors, they know what they have been told to say.

Anyone who's ever had a conversation with a cultist knows they have it down, don't they? Either from being compelled to go door to door by man-made organizations, or from outright fear that the god they serve will reject them if they don't, they are vigilant in their assault on neighborhoods worldwide. Here they come, spreading a false gospel with more zeal than we do with the real thing!

This picture is tragically wrong. We have the age-old, historic, Christian message to spread, the right and privilege to do so, and the ability to honor and obey God by taking it to *whosoever*. Why is it that cultists seem to be more effective through being forced and coerced to come to our doors with their false gospels? Perhaps our inability to communicate the basic creeds of our faith is directly related to the shirking of our responsibility to *go ye therefore* as Jesus commanded all to do in the Great Commission (Matthew 28:19-20). Perhaps our lack of knowledge is once again the main detriment.

Spreading the gospel is the responsibility of every Christian, not just the pastor or evangelist. Once we have studied, prayed, and prepared, a supernatural phenomenon takes place. It's called a smile! And a smile on the face of a Christian is certainly an act of warfare against the Devil's forces. Shouldn't it just be that way? After all, we ought to be the happiest people on earth – we're going to heaven! And shouldn't our happiness be like a bombshell to the Enemy?

Doing the actual work of evangelism, though, can heat up our spiritual battles, but it won't be a negative thing. The closeness and intimacy with God that results from sharing our faith will also bring us unexplainable and uncontrollable happiness and satisfaction. This joy seems to reproduce and will make us like a beacon of God's hope and love to a lost world. The closer we draw to God, the more yielded we become to His will, and the higher we climb on the happiness meter. Our decision to be a witness for Jesus will position us to experience what Nehemiah 8:10 proclaims – the joy of the Lord is our strength. This heaven-sent joy will result in our witness – both in lifestyle and in words – being far more effective as well. The joy we sense in doing His will spurs us on to more good works, which will replenish the joy again, causing us to continue doing His will, and so on. Remember, it starts with our decision to find our happiness in God by following the scriptural premise: *This is the day which the LORD hath made; we will rejoice and be glad in it.* Does your joy need a refreshing? If so, make the decision to start today.

Chapter 12

Shielded by Faith

Above all, taking the shield of faith, wherewith ye shall be able to quench all the fiery darts of the wicked. – Ephesians 6:16

In addition to the helmet, the people in the apostle Paul's day understood the enormous need for a strong, dependable shield. Possessing a strong shield often meant the difference between life and death. From history, we understand that the shield was not a small, insignificant thing; it was a huge, important tool. In biblical times, opposing armies often used catapults. They loaded large fireballs onto the catapults, released them, and rained blazing coals down on the enemy, setting their clothes on fire. Their huge shields protected them from these firestorms, among other perils presented during battle.

The Bible indicates that an important part of our Christian life and duty is to employ the shield of faith. It resembles the most essential ingredient in our walk with God. Is it hard to please God outside of faith? Even more than just hard, the Bible says it's impossible. And there is a difference between hard and impossible. Faith is like the glue that holds together all that we believe. We need a measure of faith to trust the Lord for salvation, to walk in His righteousness, to speak His truth, and to be His witnesses – even if it means rejection by others.

Faith or Folly?

In the modern New Age movement, visualization and a positive mental attitude have replaced faith. These mystic teachings have crept into the government school system where they are taught and practiced. Children learn to look inside themselves to find wisdom, enlightenment, and power. We should point out that any system that teaches us to look inside ourselves for these things is worldly at best and satanic at the core. Employing these practices is the next step for teachers who've been "enlightened" to New Age philosophy in colleges and universities across the land.

Having been conditioned to accept mysticism in a Western package and its bankrupt moral value system, our children have picked up the mantra of "self." They are taught that if they can think it, they can do it. They are told, "Believe it; you can achieve it." This modern replay of the old deception is actually a remnant of the once popular "mind over matter" teaching and is connected to dependence on self, not God. In an effort to improve sales, productivity, and profits, corporate officials promoted many such ideas as well, paying enormous sums for what amounted to receiving the services of familiar spirits.

Part of the legion of modern New Age gurus teach nothing more than a hybrid form of mental gymnastics, but some resort to blatant occultism, such as the voodoo practice of firewalking. Nearly every sphere of public life has been inundated by the New Age. From the military to the government, and from technology to the classroom, we see these techniques surface. Guided imagery, relaxation techniques, and spirit guides have replaced reliance on Scripture for the formula for life. Though often unbeknownst to the user, all such New Age ideas represent Satan's flimsy substitute for real biblical faith.

Remember the classic 1930s children's story, *The Little Engine That Could*? One thing to remember about that little train in the story – it isn't going anywhere without tracks. Faith is the track on which Christianity operates. We can think good thoughts and focus on positive imagery until we pass out, but any results we get without God's intervention through faith will fall short of the mark and could actually hurt our spiritual life.

Continually we become aware of motivational teachers who offer the hope of higher human potential through the techniques they sell. Many of them, some even claiming to be Christians, have borrowed their ideas straight from the pit of hell. So be careful in embracing any mental technique or practice just because it claims testimonials of success. New Age circles teach an underlying principle that we often warn audiences to avoid. Many of these techniques offer changed personalities, increased capacity for memorization or learning, elevated self-esteem, and even improved financial status for those who'll participate. Based on teaching that revolves around moral relativism and unscriptural thinking, these New Age platitudes offer little more than a satanic substitute for biblical faith.

Often, people justify these techniques based only on the results, while never considering the ethical, moral, or spiritual implications. For the Christian, we should understand that if we employ teaching or techniques based solely on the fact that they might work, we place ourselves in a compromised spiritual position at the very least. The hippies used to say, "If it feels good, do it." Now the New Agers say, "If it works, use it."

The truth is that just because something works doesn't mean it's right! Atomic bombs work; does that make them the right choice? Of course not. But today a lot of people are using techniques for self-enlightenment that are as spiritually deadly as an atomic weapon, and they are doing so just because they work.

The End and the Means

For the Christian, the end never justifies the means. God's standard is diametrically opposed to the world's system. It's the difference between the gospel of faith in God and the gospel of faith in self. Let's depart from worldly and often occult ideas and rely on pure faith in God. Stick with Scripture and God's perfect system, which allows Him to shower our lives with His blessings as we display true faith.

True faith allows us to do anything that God instructs us to do, including what man deems impossible, because nothing is impossible with God.

God is not likely to tell us to defy nature, but He requires us to believe that He is the master of our lives and the master of nature. It would be easier to walk through a wall, fly around the room, or walk on water than to think we can please God outside of faith, because without faith it is impossible to please God – not hard, *impossible*. The answers to life are not based on what we think we can do or what any occult substitute or New Age teacher may convince someone they can do. Rather, the answers are found in what God says He can do through us. This is why the apostle Paul was able to assert so confidently: *I can do all things through Christ which strengtheneth me* (Philippians 4:13). Here we see the work of the shield of faith. Stay behind it. If we do, we'll be protected from the *fiery darts of the wicked*, but once we inch away from the center point of faith, we become susceptible to Satan's deceptions.

Chapter 13

Two Big Guns: Prayer and the Word

And the sword of the Spirit, which is the word of God: Praying always with all prayer and supplication in the Spirit. – Ephesians 6:17b-18a

Prayer

The Christian has two offensive weapons in his arsenal. The first is prayer – perhaps the most potent and important element that we initiate ourselves. Prayer is the mainstay, the unseen force that undergirds all we are as believers. Without it, we are anemic and undirected by our Commander and sitting ducks for our Enemy. An old adage says, "Seven days without prayer makes one weak." How true. Prayerlessness not only weakens our spirit, but the void it creates also becomes fertile ground for the Enemy to wreak havoc, attacking our lives and homes without resistance. We might recite all the right things and be in church at every service, but if we haven't taken time to develop a strong and personal communication with the Lord, not only are our lives comparatively shallow and empty, we also are no threat to the Devil. Rather, it is the other way around.

Prayer is the hedge against running aground in the storms of life; during those intimate moments with Jesus, we see His mission and goals for our lives with clear eyes. Often, He speaks to our hearts or through His Word as we simply make the time for Him. People make the excuse that they don't have the time to pray. Their lives are so busy and have often become a picture described by the classic tract "The Tyranny of the Urgent." Instead, in a world so fraught with problems, where evil forces encroach on our homes from all sides, we simply don't have the time *not* to pray. We cannot expect to be a winner in spiritual warfare just because our name is written in the Lamb's Book of Life. Victory against a focused, vicious foe doesn't come easy; the price we pay for victory is the time, study, and effort spent in prayer.

The Weapon of Prayer

Many people do not recognize prayer as a spiritual weapon, but communication with our Lord is a real threat to Satan. If we pray in the pattern of the Bible, our prayers, through the power of God, accomplish amazing things. Captives are set free and bonds are broken from our lives and the lives of those around us by the power of God through prayer.

For example, the first thing that modern armies attempt to do is neutralize the communication centers of their adversary. Without communication, an army is in disarray, and commanders have no control over directing battles and no insight into where their enemy is or what he is doing. The Devil attempts to do this to us. He tries to knock out our communication center – our prayer.

Have you ever tried to pray for an hour? It's tough, isn't it? Besides the natural adversity our flesh displays, a myriad of roadblocks seem to stifle our prayer lives. In our busy lives today, interruptions come from every side. When we go to prayer, the children act up, the doorbell rings, our mind wanders to the other cares and chores that need attention, and all sorts of other distractions take place. Sound familiar?

For the ladies, your prayer might go like this:

"Okay, Lord, I'm going to pray for an hour.

"Dear Lord, I thank you that you are the bread of life. Bread ... and I need milk too. Oh, and I've got to bake a cake for that church social next week."

Have you ever done that, ladies? And men aren't any better; they might pray like this:

"Okay, Lord, I'm going to pray for an hour.

"Dear Lord, I thank you that you are the light of the world. Light ... you know the light in the garage has been burned out for about two weeks now, and now that I think about it, I haven't seen my tools. God, I'm going to tan my boy's hide when I get home!"

Now that may be a little more scattered and comical than what actually happens during our times of prayer, but we know that anyone who has attempted to begin an active prayer life can relate.

There is no doubt that when we go to pray, Satan goes to work trying to scramble our communications. His objective is to cut us off from God completely if he can. He wants to disable us at all costs. Our Enemy knows that prayer is an offensive weapon, one that presents the gravest of threats to his kingdom. We had better realize it as well.

Until I (Eric) got a plan for prayer straight in my mind before commencing, prayer times were maybe fifteen minutes followed by a nap! Just as with spiritual warfare in general, having a plan, a formula for prayer, helps. Before we can go to battle in prayer, we need to establish a strong "beachhead" of regular communion with God. The example the Lord gave us in Matthew 6:9-13 is best, and is known commonly as the Lord's Prayer:

> After this manner therefore pray ye: Our Father which art in heaven, Hallowed be thy name. Thy kingdom come, Thy will be done in earth, as it is in heaven. Give us this day our daily bread. And forgive us our debts, as we forgive our debtors. And lead us not into temptation, but deliver us from evil: For thine is the kingdom, and the power, and the glory, for ever. Amen.

Capsulated in these five verses are some of the most powerful, life-changing teachings in the entire Bible. Virtually everything we need in life can be seen in the transparency of Jesus' words here. Fully absorbing what is taught in Matthew 6:9-13 has been the subject of many great and thorough books, so we won't try to cover all of it. Suffice it to say, the subject of prayer is an important element in either our victory or our defeat.

In fact, without an ongoing, active, daily prayer life, is there really any proof of our Christianity? How can we claim to love Him, yet exclude speaking to Him and allowing Him full access to communicate with us for extended periods on a regular basis?

Remember when you accepted Jesus as Savior of your life? How did you do it? You prayed. Now, we need to examine our prayer life again. If it is nonexistent, we need to search out the reasons why. The Bible exhorts us to examine ourselves to see if we are *in the faith* (2 Corinthians 13:5). An old saying applies here: "There's no time like the present." Spiritual battles in these last days will not be won by riding along on yesterday's prayers, yesterday's anointing, or yesterday's good intentions. Satan is coming after the church with both barrels blazing, and unless we are "prayed up," we're going to pay a price. Better to consider this question now than to wait until it's too late. If a person is not engaged in intimate times of fellowship with God, there really is no tangible evidence that he or she has truly converted to Christianity.

Afraid to Pray?

Being open to God's direction through prayers and Bible study is a matter of lordship. It may be that many of us steer clear from getting too personal with God for fear that He might meddle in our lives. That may sound strange to some who commune with God regularly, but the closer we get to God, the more He speaks to us, and the more He speaks, the more He directs our paths (Psalm 37:23). Sounds great, right? Definitely, unless we aren't willing to relinquish control of our life to God.

We know it's not popular to say this in today's society fraught with New Age relativism, but the truth is that man has always wanted to be his own god, and things are no different today. We want to live by our own rules and meet our own standards. This caused the rebellion in the garden (Genesis 3), and Satan still achieves his will in the lives of humankind by understanding and using this factor. For the world, it's a matter of self and greed. Sadly, it's the same for the Christian. That's right, except we call it "lordship issues" when referring to brethren who do not allow the Lord to deal with issues of the flesh. The "gospel of self" keeps many Christians mired in the same muck as the world around us. The work of this powerful spirit has captured many millions and made them captive to Satan's old lie with fresh paint on it called the New Age movement.

We know that some Christians today purposely stay away from intimate times of prayer, because God reveals His desired changes in our lifestyles and brings His conviction to bear on our hearts during such times. But thankfully, with God, change is good. He'll never convict and convince us of the need for any change that's not in our best interest. And He'll never ask us to surrender anything to Him that He won't replace with something so much better, complete with His blessing. How tragic that we would attempt to live by our own means and try to keep God at bay, just to hold on to some activity, practice, or lifestyle. This attitude always ends with us on the losing end. So to position ourselves to win in spiritual warfare and in life itself, prayer is the key.

The Word of God

As vital as prayer is to the life of a Christian, it would be misguided at best unless we know how and to whom we are praying. God, in His forethought, saw fit to make certain that mankind would have the opportunity to know who He is, what He did, and how to communicate with Him. Therefore, over a fifteen-hundred-year period, using the mind and pen of over forty different individuals, many of whom never knew one another, God gave men His Word. This wonderful, living document, captured within sixty-six different books, is bound together now as "The Holy Bible."

Scripture tells us that the Word of God is a sharp, powerful two-edged sword (Hebrews 4:12). It is a weapon of warfare (Ephesians 6:17b). However, it does more than that. In the context of spiritual warfare, we sometimes only think of the Bible as a weapon against the Enemy. But that is getting the cart before the horse. Our personal growth through reading, memorizing, and living out the truths of the Bible make it possible for us to be effective warriors doing battle against the forces of darkness. As we study the Bible, letting it sink into our hearts, it acts as a supernatural medicine, not only to our spirit, but to our mental and physical lives as well. Our growth in God is always in direct correlation to the amount of time we spend in the pages of the Bible.

We can always make a connection between weak, confused Christians whose lives reflect no victory and whose devotional lives have fallen into disrepair. When this happens, our spiritual compass begins to read inaccurately, blurring our ability to navigate the treacherous seas of life without incident. Just as the Bible points out, it's a two-edged sword. One edge is always facing us, working on the rough edges, honing us into the powerful people God intends us to be, lighting our path, and illuminating our minds and hearts. This is the real and original "soul food." Satan is terrorized by the believer who knows the Word of God and constantly nourishes his soul with it. For the Christian to be effective in spiritual battles, he must have gone through the basic training of the Scriptures.

Knowing this to be true, if you were the Devil, wouldn't you do everything possible to discredit the Bible? Of course. Look around today and notice how often we hear the secular world attack the Bible as antiquated, as just a book of stories, or as being altered and unreliable. It is no wonder that Satan has manipulated fallen mankind to cast such ugly aspersions on God's Word. He has a great advantage by bringing doubts and questions concerning the Bible because, if it is unreliable, Christianity falls apart. New Agers say it's been doctored; atheists claim it's nothing but fairy tales. Yet God Himself has declared it as alive and has proven so through repeated fulfillment of prophecy. Many men have set out to disprove the Bible, only to become its avid defenders in the process. Scientists have scoffed at it, only to turn to it later for answers.

The Bible gives us the ability to know who the Enemy is and details of his forces that we need to effectively wage spiritual warfare. It is not a book of philosophy. We cannot defeat the Devil with philosophy. He's always going to have the upper hand with anyone who does so. We simply cannot reason with the powers of hell. Aside from utilizing what is taught in the Bible, there is only defeat – one way or another. Satan always begins by first trying to defeat us in our mind. This is why the *washing of water by the word* and the *renewing of your mind* through the cleansing process of Scripture study is so vital. Without it, can we really assert, *I can do all things through Christ* or *we are more than conquerors?*

Many will ignore God's precious, life-giving Word, but what about those who do read it and still don't place their trust in God? The reasons may vary, but two factors stand out. First, our fallen nature entices us to guide our own ship and live our lives, as sinful as they may be, our way. Secondly, the Bible tells us that *the god of this world* has blinded the eyes of the lost (2 Corinthians 4:4). Whether it's to argue with the authenticity of Scripture or to never read it at all, Satan wants men to be aloof from its real purpose and content.

Dear Christian, he wants the same for us. He knows there is power and life within its pages, and that every human who reads it and receives the Savior revealed within it is a potential threat to his dark kingdom. Satan also knows that the Bible is a legal document – the most important one of all time. He understands perfectly that he is able to do only as much as the Father allows him. When going about *seeking whom he may devour* (1 Peter 5:8), one of the Devil's main emphases is to work wherever we are ignorant. He is poised to take his step-by-step destruction right through the open door of unknowing.

If we do not know our own rights and authority in Jesus, and the abilities and rights that Satan has to kill, steal, and destroy (John 10:10), then we are bound to live in jeopardy. Moreover, if we walk in spiritual blindness, we are destined to live incomplete and powerless lives, reflecting less than the victory that Jesus' blood purchased for us. The result is that our homes and families are at peril and our witness is often anemic and ineffective.

To repeat, the Bible tells us that certain attitudes and actions can open us up to spiritual attack. For example, in 2 Corinthians 2:10-11, the apostle Paul notes that unforgiveness can be an inroad for the Enemy to use in his warfare against us. He warns the Corinthians that they are not to be unaware of the Devil's devices and schemes. The King James Version uses the word *ignorant*. Paul is talking to Christians here and asserts that Satan can get an advantage over us if we are ignorant and disobedient to God's precepts. No, we are not talking about demon possession, but we are talking about disabling some aspect of our lives through the sin of unforgiveness and through lack of understanding. We venture to say that millions of believers are suffering at Satan's hand today from simple ignorance of God's Word.

If we are going to please God, we must know His guidelines for life. And if we are to be any sort of challenge to Satan and his army of evil, we must know who we are as God's ambassadors, and know our legal rights in the spirit realm. We guarantee that Satan knows his. He is a legal expert and will use our lack of knowledge against us (Hosea 4:6). When we wield the sword of the Spirit, we must do so accurately and with the force of the sound doctrinal power reflected in the pages of God's Word.

Chapter 14

The Battle Cry of Praise

Let the high praises of God be in their mouth, and a two-edged sword in their hand. – Psalm 149:6

Christians know that mankind was created expressly to have fellowship with God. Part of that fellowship is predicated upon our worship of Him. Though certainly worship is more than just musical, we know how important music is to the Lord. When we study the Scriptures, we notice many verses instructing us on the subject of music. One of the best known is this one from Paul's letter to the Colossians.

Let the word of Christ dwell in you richly in all wisdom; teaching and admonishing one another in psalms and hymns and spiritual songs, singing with grace in your hearts to the Lord. And whatsoever ye do in word or deed, do all in the name of the Lord Jesus, giving thanks to God and the Father by him.
– Colossians 3:16-17

This passage gives us a microcosmic overview of God's desire for the operation of our lives, as Paul lays out God's will concerning music. Whatever we do, we are to do it for God's glory. Is it any wonder then that the adversary would manipulate music to derail praise from God and deceive man into directing it toward himself?

Controversy

Though the Bible is replete with passages dealing with music, praise, worship, songs, psalmists, and musical instruments, most saints are amazed to find nearly nine hundred Scripture passages that deal directly with music. In all of those verses, God neither advocates nor forbids any particular instrument, sound, or type of music. It would have been so much simpler if God had declared a favorite style, but He didn't. This fact adds to the discussion of this often-divisive topic within Christian circles, but nonetheless it adds to the absolute imperative reason that we should study this issue with great care. We wish that God would just issue a weekly "Top Ten," but since He doesn't, we'll each just have to dig in and search the Scriptures on this one.

More Controversy

Music can probably fall into three categories: first, music that is devoid of serving God; next, music that is neutral of serving God; and finally, music that is aimed squarely at serving Him. Christians find very limited agreement about music, but we can probably find agreement that some lyrics and lifestyles being promulgated in music today are antibiblical. Some lyrics could perhaps be classified as passive or neutral, neither glorifying God nor breaking any particular biblical standards. Thankfully, many lyrics and lifestyles are glorifying to the Lord and blessed by Him.

We recognize that music is perhaps one of the most hotly contested topics of discussion among Christians today and certainly requires a much more in-depth debate than we'll allow for here. We've been around and around from every angle on this issue, and without ample space, we know we're leaving this spiritual lightning rod dangling in the wind. Regardless of all the controversies, if we stick with the Bible, we can be certain whether the lyrics and lifestyle being presented are valid and worthy to be called "Christian."

Most importantly, we can be assured that God has a perfect will concerning music – that He be worshiped and glorified through it. That kind of music becomes an effective weapon in the arsenal of an informed believer.

A clear example of how God honors music that is played and sung for His complete glory can be seen in the overwhelming outpouring of His Spirit during the consecration of Solomon's temple in 2 Chronicles 5. As the musicians and singers worshiped the Lord, the temple was filled with the glory cloud of God, and God literally overtook the participants. Since the New Testament tells us that we (His church) are now the temple of God, it would make sense that all believers who want God's anointing will fill His temple with music that brings Him honor and praise. Why would we ever want to settle for anything less?

Secular Music – Satan's Battle Cry?

While we don't want to get sidetracked too far here, it's very hard to resist a few comments concerning the toll that ungodly secular music is exacting in our day.

We have concentrated many years of ministry and thousands of hours of research and effort on exposing the darkness within today's music industry. Coming from a past in which I was caught in the grips of the music business as a performer, record producer, and recording engineer, I (Eric) have personally experienced the worldly attraction brought on by the lure of rock music. Both of us have written, spoken, and ministered about this issue in great depth, and one thing we have concluded is that what the world is offering up for young people and adults to listen to today is laced with spiritual poison. The accompanying lifestyle the musicians present is of as much or more concern, because music plays such a pivotal part in so many lives now. From rap to rock and from pop to country, the music industry is generally at odds with the overwhelming scriptural evidence as to why music exists at all. This brings us back to the reason we've included this chapter.

Music As a Weapon of War

"Praise and worship" is more than singing hymns and choruses on Sunday morning. Lifting our voices to God is not only an obedient expression of our love and awe for God; it is also a powerful tool of spiritual warfare.

To define the differences, praise is usually sung about God to men. Praise edifies, teaches, exhorts, and encourages. Worship, on the other hand, is usually sung directly to God. Worship praises God, thanks Him, adores Him, and petitions Him. To those who understand what the Scripture reveals about praise, and who know what is happening in the spirit realm as we carry on worship, the term *praise and worship* truly becomes a battle cry.

> *But thou art holy, O thou that inhabitest the praises
> of Israel.* – Psalm 22:3

Scripture says that God inhabits or is enthroned in the very praises of His people. What an awesome thought! The King of all creation is magnified and lives in our praises! Dare we hold back giving Him glory whenever and wherever we can?

In Psalm 22:3, the English word *inhabitest* is translated from the Greek word *Yashab*. It literally means "to sit," "to remain," or "to have one's abode." This is extraordinarily powerful when we realize what this means to us as we do battle with the Devil.

To give praise to God is truly a spiritual experience. God, the Spirit, dwells in our worship. Do you suppose He knows immediately when our worship is phony, contrived, and not truly from the heart? No one should believe that God ever honors a lackadaisical, halfhearted worshiper. We see a key to this in John 4:24 when Jesus states: *God is a Spirit: and they that worship him must worship him in spirit and in truth.*

Notice Jesus doesn't say, "Those that worship Him *should* worship Him in spirit and in truth." He said *must.* Otherwise, our unclean offering is void of the presence, comfort, and power of God. Without the Holy Spirit's anointing as we stand in His truthful righteousness, our words are empty and our actions meaningless, for God longs for and only inhabits the true praise of His people.

Is it any wonder that Satan tries to intimidate men in their praise and worship to almighty God? He knows that not only is it a point of obedience for Christians to unabashedly worship God, but if he can keep them from doing so, they'll also be much less a threat to his evil work. In saying these things, we are not promoting demonstrative displays that bring attention to humans in the name of worship. But if Satan can cause us to fear what men think and keep us from entering into God's courts through praise, how much more will he be able to accomplish as he whips us in spiritual warfare? The Devil does this for good reason, for without the weapon of praise and a complete understanding of what it accomplishes in the spirit realm, we are greatly hampered in our effectiveness in battle.

We don't pretend to know all the dynamics that take place spiritually when a Christian worships the Lord, but we do know that something powerful, something extremely potent, takes place. We're not referring to a feeling we might receive while worshiping. Though emotions might come into play during worship, the tears we may shed are not the benchmark for how effective our worship may have been. The cogency of our worship is found in the binding and even outright confusion our praise brings against the forces of evil.

Setting the Table for Battle

In 2 Chronicles 20, we read of Israel facing overwhelming odds as they prepared for battle with three alien armies. In worldly terms, the battle looked as if it were over before it began, with Israel meeting disaster. We all seem to reach a point in our lives with a mountain before us that looks insurmountable. In the case of Israel, though, defeat meant captivity by their foes and probably death. Greatly outnumbered, the army of Israel appeared to be doomed. In the natural realm, things looked bad, but all things are possible with God.

The night before the battle, God's Spirit came upon the Levite Jahaziel with a great word of prophecy.

> *Hearken ye, all Judah, and ye inhabitants of Jerusalem, and thou king Jehoshaphat, Thus saith the* LORD *unto you, Be not afraid nor dismayed by reason of this great multitude; for the battle is not yours, but God's. To morrow go ye down against them: behold, they come up by the cliff of Ziz; and ye shall find them at the end of the brook, before the wilderness of Jeruel. Ye shall not need to fight in this battle: set yourselves, stand ye still, and see the salvation of the* LORD *with you, O Judah and Jerusalem: fear not, nor be dismayed; to morrow go out against them: for the* LORD *will be with you.* – 2 Chronicles 20:15-17

This is exactly the kind of word we want from the Lord when facing the impossible, isn't it? The passage says that Jehoshaphat and all of Israel worshiped the Lord, some probably kneeling, some bowing, and some lying prostrate before Him. We also see here that, being led by the Levites, some stood and praised God *with a loud voice*. (When the chips are down, even the most conservative worshipers just may shout to the Lord!)

The next morning, Jehoshaphat appointed *singers unto the* L ORD to go out before the army to worship the Lord. After this, the Lord set ambushes against their enemies. As God's people worshiped and sang, the enemy armies slew each other. This is a picture or "type" of what can happen in the spirit realm during spiritual warfare. Wow! We don't have to paint much more of a picture than that to demonstrate the victory available to us when we honestly and earnestly give praise to God in song. Worship sets the table for victory. These people were in a very serious life-threatening situation. There was no pretense in their praise. It was honest and without reservation. And true to His Word, God *inhabited the praises of Israel*.

In 2 Chronicles 20, Scripture goes on to say that Jehoshaphat and the Israelites took great loads of treasure, jewels, and other spoil and returned to Jerusalem the same way they had gone to battle – worshiping with psalteries, harps, and trumpets.

Verse 29 says *the fear of God* was on all the countries surrounding Israel, and peace and safety filled the land during Jehoshaphat's reign. Could it be that peace, safety, and provision are attainable for those who worship God in spirit and in truth?

To Praise or Not to Praise

Too often, we see people concentrating on how they feel during worship. Some saints seem to enter a worship service waiting on God to miraculously touch them before they begin to sing and enter into the flow of the service. They seem to be waiting on the worship leader and musicians to play just the right song that touches their feelings. May we say that whether we feel like it or not, we are commanded to worship God. We need to enter in and concentrate on Him, allowing how we feel (be it good or mediocre) to become secondary. Often we may not feel anything as we begin to sing and praise the Lord. But as we do, His Spirit comes and meets us, filling our hearts with His joy as we express our devotion to Him. And let us not forget the biblical examples we have, which tell us music is indeed an integral part of the battle in the spirit. Perhaps we could say that it may be a dangerous thing to just stand around week in and week out while a corporate worship service is going on. Would any worshiper have done that in the wilderness of Tekoa (2 Chronicles 20)?

We do recognize the excesses within the body of Christ, as some in the church seem to actually "worship" worship itself, by using mere human effort to work themselves into a state of "spirituality." It is also troublesome that in some corners of Christianity, the preaching of the Word and the ministry of the saints have been neglected to some extent because of the overemphasis on musical presentation. Still, while we're more concerned with the spiritual lack apparent in those who never enter into worship than with those who are perhaps on the opposite extreme, the church must understand the paramount importance of personal and corporate worship. Here's why.

The Unseen Reason for Praise

As we study and learn what the Word of God says about worship, we recognize that while we are lifting praise and worship to heaven, a second, unseen benefit is taking place.

As we read Scripture, and in particular see the Old Testament "types" about how music and worship were used, we see that New Testament worship is indeed a weapon of spiritual warfare. Just as the application and appropriation of the blood of the Lamb covers and protects us today, our understanding of what is taking place in the spirit realm as we praise God is integral to our victory as well. It could be said that the Christian who knows the havoc that his or her worship to God is wreaking on the powers of darkness will endeavor to worship God with all the more vigor. In fact, it is the glory of the saints to inflict damage on the Devil and his workers.

In Psalm 149, we see a terrific picture of both the purpose and priorities of worship.

> *Praise ye the* LORD. *Sing unto the* LORD *a new song, and his praise in the congregation of saints.*
>
> *Let Israel rejoice in him that made him: let the children of Zion be joyful in their King.*
>
> *Let them praise his name in the dance: let them sing praises unto him with the timbrel and harp.*
>
> *For the* LORD *taketh pleasure in his people: he will beautify the meek with salvation.*
>
> *Let the saints be joyful in glory: let them sing aloud upon their beds.*
>
> *Let the high praises of God be in their mouth, and a two-edged sword in their hand;*
>
> *To execute vengeance upon the heathen, and punishments upon the people;*
>
> *To bind their kings with chains, and their nobles with fetters of iron;*
>
> *To execute upon them the judgment written: this honour have all his saints. Praise ye the* LORD.

Notice the first five verses portray our foremost obligation in worship – to give God glory. But beginning in verse 6, we see the secondary priority come into play – warfare against the Enemy. In reading Old Testament passages, we are to view them through New Testament eyes. Knowing that, and knowing that our battle is not against flesh and blood but against the principalities and powers of hell, what we see here is a clear mission for the church today. We are to praise God, taking up the sharp and powerful sword of the Word of God; and through our scriptural praise, we inflict damage on the Devil's kingdom.

To proclaim the judgment of almighty God upon the Devil's forces is an honor; and as one modern version of the Bible says, *this is the glory of all his faithful people* (Psalm 149:9b NIV). Remember this passage the next time you sing, "There is power, power, wonder-working power in the blood of the Lamb." Not only are we lifting up Jesus and giving Him the glory He is due, but by our commitment to worship, we are also punishing, weakening, and dethroning demonic beings who have designs on taking more captives around our general area.

If *one should chase a thousand, and two put ten thousand to flight* (Deuteronomy 32:30), just imagine what damage we could inflict upon the Enemy's kingdom in our locale if we joined together in the understanding that our praises weaken the defenses and advancements of the powers of darkness.

One more thought: if you've wondered why the usual, historical worship service in churches begins and ends with song, now you know. Just as Jehoshaphat sent the singers and musicians out at the head of the army and also worshiped God after the battle, we do the same today. This is also reflected in the Lord's Prayer, in which Jesus taught us how to pray by both beginning (Matthew 6:9b) and ending (Matthew 6:13b) with praise and worship. A solid, vibrant worship service softens the hard soil in the heart to accept the preaching of God's Word and binds the spiritual forces intent on deterring the will of God.

Praise Your Way to Freedom

"I just don't feel like worshiping God. Things are coming unglued in my life and I have too many troubles to deal with." Though a Christian may not ever verbalize these words, it is probably too often the scenario.

Let us say that any saint who is experiencing life's turmoil or spiritual oppression is the very person who needs more than anyone else to begin to praise God. When the storms of life hit, instead of giving in to the human inclination to declare, "Woe is me," and drifting into depression and despair, our reaction should be to praise the Lord. Do we praise Him because of the problem? No, we worship Him because He has all of the help and solutions we need in the midst of life's problems. Satan desires us to depend on human means to overcome the perils of this life. God desires us to look to Him instead. The Devil desires for us to fall into the trap of depression, but God says, "Come unto Me if you are weary and burdened!"

> *Be careful for nothing; but in every thing by prayer and supplication with thanksgiving let your requests be made known unto God. And the peace of God, which passeth all understanding, shall keep your hearts and minds through Christ Jesus.*
> – Philippians 4:6-7

If we are looking for real answers to the storms of life, we need to turn to prayer and supplication (worship) as Scripture exhorts, and receive the peace of God. Why do anything else?

Worry or Worship?

We cannot honestly lift worship to God and worry at the same time. That is so freeing we'll repeat it again. It is impossible to worship and worry at the same time. Worry and worship are mutually exclusive activities. We can't participate in both simultaneously. In the gospel accounts, time and again, Jesus told His followers to *take no thought* for things like food and shelter. He was saying, "Don't worry."

Do you suppose, if we do something that Jesus told us not to do, that in doing so we sin? Of course. Besides, what did worry ever accomplish? Someone once said that worry is like a rocking chair; it's something to do, but it won't get you anywhere. Worry wears us down. Worship lifts us up. Worry embodies Satan's will, while worship of God enthrones Him in our circumstances. If we are under attack and our situation has the aroma of prune soup, remember: Praise breaks the back of Satan's attacks. It may not be an instant solution, but it will certainly be the right action to take.

So may we suggest that the next time tests emerge and the trials of life seem insurmountable, make the volitional choice to turn to God in joyful praise. The Enemy is confounded and God is glorified. Plus, we become a powerful witness to those around us as we walk through the trials with an attitude of praise, giving God the glory for His strength in us.

What Kind of Praise?

O Lord our Lord, how excellent is thy name in all the earth! who hast set thy glory above the heavens.

Out of the mouth of babes and sucklings hast thou ordained strength because of thine enemies, that thou mightest still the enemy and the avenger.
– Psalm 8:1-2

With all the talk in this chapter about praise, it would be good to close with a biblical definition of just what that means. Here in Psalm 8:2, the word *strength* appears in the King James Version. It is the Hebrew word *oze* (*Strong's Exhaustive Concordance* #05797). The English translation in *Strong's* rendered for this word is "force, security, strength, strong, power, boldness, loud, mighty, majesty, praise." These are words that describe the kind of worship God desires. If we go into battle with praise that fits this description flowing from our lips, we are certain to walk in the victory of God while we displace the Enemy.

Chapter 15

What Then Must We Do?

I have fought a good fight, I have finished my course, I have kept the faith: Henceforth there is laid up for me a crown of righteousness, which the Lord, the righteous judge, shall give me at that day: and not to me only, but unto all them also that love his appearing.
– 2 Timothy 4:7-8

Getting to the Kingdom

Much of spiritual warfare is fought in the mind as a tussle of ideologies and will. Scripture indicates that bringing our minds into subjection to God's Word is a lifelong struggle. For some of us, the battle may be more intense. For others, surrendering to His will and commands may be somewhat less demanding. But for all of us, it is worth it.

Scripture tells us in 2 Corinthians 10:4-5 that we are to pull down strongholds, imaginations, and thoughts, and make them subject to Christ. Satan's strategy in trying to make us wilt in the heat of battle cannot succeed if we know the Word of God and are willing to follow it. The Bible indicates that it shouldn't surprise us when trials and afflictions come our way. Peter speaks to us about this in 1 Peter 4:12-13:

> *Beloved, think it not strange concerning the fiery*
> *trial which is to try you, as though some strange*
> *thing happened unto you: But rejoice, inasmuch as*
> *ye are partakers of Christ's sufferings; that, when*
> *his glory shall be revealed, ye may be glad also with*
> *exceeding joy.*

When trials come our way, we need to remember who is on our side and what He has sent us to accomplish here. Some things are important to remember in times of spiritual struggle:

> The battle is not really ours but God's. We are but a willing conduit for His power to be manifested through. God knows every thought, every fear, and every strength. Nothing will take Him by surprise. We serve under His protection (Psalm 91).

> The weapons for victory are not our own. They are made available and are empowered by God. None are more powerful than the knowledge of His Word coupled with the blood of the cross (Revelation 12:11).

> Worldly means will not bring spiritual victory. Our focus must be on His purpose and power (2 Corinthians 10:3-4).

> Make a cognizant, resolute decision that no ungodly communication shall flow into or out of us. Double-mindedness spells defeat (2 Corinthians 6:14-18; 7:1; James 1:8; Hebrews 11:6).

What If You or Your House Is Under Attack?

Often we are asked questions such as, "What do I do if my family is under spiritual attack?" "What steps do I take if my children are seeing 'things' in their rooms?" "Demonic forces are assaulting my body and mind. How can I stop them?"

This book contains some good, practical information to help win these kinds of battles. Let's review some of it.

Perhaps the most important things we can do within our own control are to renew our minds through study in the Word of God, to build up our spirit man through prayer and praise to God, and to diligently seek to *guard* our Christian walk. Taking proactive, preventative steps such as the simple recognition that we are all soldiers in the spiritual war helps give us a decisive advantage. As we pointed out early on, Satan is looking for those that he *can* devour (1 Peter 5:8). This indicates that there are some he *can't* devour. Those ignorant and unaware of who they truly are in Christ Jesus and those unknowledgeable as to how the Enemy operates are likely to be Satan's primary targets for attack. Being cognizant that a real, formidable foe is loose, and that this foe is focused on wreaking havoc inside the body of Christ is a healthy realization for all believers to remember. Satan has a strategy and so must we. Being alert and on guard is part of having the kind of close, personal faith that carries us through rough waters and helps bulletproof our lives, leaving less room for the Enemy to gain access. Are we suggesting paranoia and fear? Of course not. The knowledge of an adversary is the first step to defeat it, but for anyone not completely surrendered to the King of Kings, we need to reiterate: there is no victory in spiritual warfare without an ongoing, repentant relationship with Jesus Christ. Anything less, and we're powerless easy pickings' for Satan.

Authentic Repentance

An overriding theme in these pages has been repentance followed by appropriate biblical actions. Please note that repentance isn't complete if we only experience godly sorrow for wrong deeds, words, and thoughts. Repentance should move us to action, which includes applying God's principles in our lives as we seek to follow His path. If Satan can keep us bound in a cycle of sin and guilt, followed by only *acknowledging* our failures to God, we'll be riders on hell's sinister merry-go-round simply repeating the same again and again – but never really finding actual freedom. The key to breaking this cycle is recognizing that true repentance is agreeing with God and taking steps to avoid whatever Satan is using to ensnare us on his treadmill.

One of the best first steps in breaking out of the personal prison many seemed confined in is to become accountable to a *mature and trustworthy* believer or believers. To some incarcerated by guilt and shame, this in itself is a frightening proposition. But James 5:16 reveals to us a promise of freedom if we'll just step out by faith and trust God for the results. It says, *Confess your faults one to another, and pray one for another, that ye may be healed. The effectual fervent prayer of a righteous man availeth much.* It may be an intimidating, even scary thing to follow this verse, but it clearly states that if we confess and pray, then we *will* be healed. Satan has had his ugly way with many a Christian who could not bring themselves to confess their needs and failures to others. The body of Christ isn't really what God intended if we allow fear or shame to keep us in the dark bondage of silence. When we come out of the shadows and call out for help, God assures us of peace and healing. Just follow His Word and see for yourself.

Defeating Addictions

Many Christians have privately indicated that they feel like they can never be free, especially when dealing with addictions. Addictions, destructive patterns of practice and/or thought, come in many shapes and sizes. When a person comes to faith in Christ, they positionally become new creatures in Christ (2 Corinthians 5:17-21). In other words, no matter who we've been, what we've done, or how we feel, we are new creatures in Christ Jesus because of His finished work on Calvary and our simple trust in Him. However, this wonderful fact doesn't magically make all of our troubles disappear. Also, we can be tricked by trusting our emotions or feelings, which might change from day to day or even moment to moment. The world, the flesh, and the Devil can certainly still tug at believers regardless of the truth that our eternal destination has changed from hell to heaven. In fact, experience dictates that Satan may even step up his assaults as we purpose to walk ahead with God seemingly *because* he's lost us to the Savior. This seems to ring especially true to those who've been an addict of one kind or another.

Some experience God's supernatural and often instantaneous hand of deliverance from addictions (such as Eric did from a fourteen-year addiction to drugs in 1981). For others, it is not always so simple. When addicts come to Christ, it's important that they fill their minds and hearts with God's Word and that they purpose to make changes in the surroundings and associations that may have influenced and abetted their addictions. Out of necessity, this is what Eric did, even leaving his occupation and security as a recording engineer and record producer because he knew he just could not continue to be in what was a volatile and drug-filled environment. (* Read or download Eric's powerful testimony at *www.ericbarger.com*.) Here again, accountability is crucial, as is wise guidance, counsel, and lots of prayer. There is much more to say on this important issue but regardless of the time and effort needed to find freedom, the fact is that God is a loving, delivering Creator who is able to meet every need and set every captive free!

Though some want to just debate the fine points of theology concerning this, there can be times of intense struggle that genuinely born-again people experience as they persevere to walk with the Lord. Many in today's society come into relationship with Christ with some overwhelming life challenges, including patterns of addiction. Those who are critical of others' struggles should beware that their lack of mercy may be rooted in spiritual pride, and the Bible clearly states that pride leads to destruction (Proverbs 16:18). You see, it's not what addictions or practices may still exist in the life or mind of a person at the point of their new birth, but it's where their new life in Christ can lead them. For a new believer, it's paramount that first they understand that by faith they have passed from eternal death to eternal life whether they feel like it or not. Next comes the task of confronting the ungodly addictions or patterns that they lived in before surrendering to Christ. This is certainly one pivotal place where the rubber really meets the road, as we learn to depend on Jesus' strength and power and upon the authority of God's Word, even though the changes aren't always instantaneous.

When one comes to Christ for salvation and receives His forgiveness for their sins, they typically don't have much of the understanding of what is waiting up ahead in their spiritual future. Don't we all wish that every powerful truth found in the Bible just entered us through spiritual osmosis when we are born again? But it doesn't work that way. Learning, abiding, and living in God is a lifelong progression that really has no conclusion no matter when in life we begin the journey.

When Satan commences an attack on a new believer (or one who doesn't understand our biblical responsibility to resist him), it can feel like being sideswiped by an eighteen-wheeler.

Here we are, trying to walk with God, and out of nowhere the Enemy uses a circumstance, situation, or perhaps something from our past and we find ourselves thinking or doing things completely out of line with God's will and where we want to go with Him. Occasions like this can devastate the new and often fragile confidence of baby saints. At that early stage of spiritual development, most do not recognize that Satan's will for our Christian life hasn't changed since we've gotten saved. His job description is still to kill, steal, and destroy, and perhaps we've given the Devil a foothold to operate in our lives and nobody has told us of Paul's warning about this from Ephesians chapter 4. When you are facing these skirmishes in the spiritual war, it is wonderful to know the eternal truth found in 2 Corinthians 5:17 which says, *Therefore if any man be in Christ, he is a new creature: old things are passed away; behold, all things are become new.* Knowing that we are indeed conquerors in Him, and reminding ourselves and the adversary that *neither death, nor life, nor angels, nor principalities, nor powers, nor things present, nor things to come, Nor height, nor depth, nor any other creature, shall be able to separate us from the love of God, which is in Christ Jesus our Lord* (Romans 8:38-39), is one of the most powerful things we can do. *But it doesn't necessarily alleviate the shock of the attack and our human failure to withstand it.*

Improving our ability to resist Satan's lures is a matter of growing in knowledge about God's Word and His doctrines and principles, and also in our ability at any given time to recognize and hear the Holy Spirit as He guides, convicts, and speaks to our hearts. We are all in various stages of understanding about God and life in Him, and, as we see reflected in the apostle Paul's admonitions to the believers at Corinth, habits often fueled by the power of the flesh can and do still haunt genuine Christians. That is not an excuse. It's just a fact. But as God, the most loving of Fathers, directs and instructs us, it surely doesn't have to be the final outcome. If your name is written in the Book of Life, peace and freedom ARE available to you. Persevere

Now, About Your House ...

The Enemy can and will use various means to gain an advantage over us and the members of our family. Even though many Christians have the mistaken impression that their homes and possessions are off limits for Lucifer's workers, this theory is as flawed as to believe the Devil doesn't exist in the first place!

As we've enumerated in speaking in churches and conferences, in our various teaching materials, and in this book, though the Devil may have lost your soul eternally, his plan for your earthly life has not changed. It's in his printed job description to kill, steal, and destroy (John 10:10). As we've stated, Satan understands that if he can keep us occupied with problems *internally*, then we are not likely to focus on or as successfully fulfill the gospel's Great Commission *externally* out in the world.

Perhaps the most effective inroad Satan has into the homes of Christians is through ignorance. A thorough study of the warnings of Hosea 4:6 is in order here. The next effective trap is disobedience, as residents fall into idolatry, endearing themselves to ideology and/or physical items that oppose the will, plan, and purpose of God. Sometimes even that which appears to be the most innocuous and innocent can prove to be just what Satan needs to divert our attention from God and the principles found in His Word. Here, we ascribe to the model of vigilance but not paranoia as we stand guard against the Enemy's subtle advances.

What objects or items may have made their way into your home that could be giving Satan room and right to operate? Each of these authors has counseled many moms, dads, teens, and children concerning this question. Many times the demonic

WHAT THEN MUST WE DO?

access point into their homes has proven to be some physical item or idolatrous affection by one or more of the residents. Books, games, toys, music, movies, and the like have inflicted damage on the spiritual atmosphere, freedom, and lives of the people there, all because they have given the demonic a legal foothold. Religious artifacts, and of course obvious occult or New Age objects and entanglements, are certain paths for demonic intrusion as well.

Please take note of the account recorded in Acts 19 as Paul ministered at Ephesus. Eric and David have given this great example for many years when ministering about the world of the occult.

The story in Acts 19 is one laden with great insight and also warning for believers. Coming on the heels of the Holy Spirit displaying great might and power through Paul's ministry (vv. 11-12), and the account of the seven unsaved Jewish exorcists being physically beaten by a possessed man (vv. 13-16), the whole region was awash with interest and awe of God and the display of His sovereign power in Jesus' name (v. 17).

Next, Acts 19:18-20 records: *And many that believed came, and confessed, and shewed their deeds. Many of them also which used curious arts brought their books together, and burned them before all men: and they counted the price of them, and found it fifty thousand pieces of silver. So mightily grew the word of God and prevailed.*

Did you catch that? Under the conviction of the Holy Spirit *believers* confessed and renounced their evil deeds and surrendered idolatrous items before the Lord.

What stands out here is:

> The Spirit of God was moving as Paul operated in ministry.

> These were Christians who confessed and severed

ties with that which Satan had previously used in their lives.

> Earthly value or financial worth was not of consequence to the Ephesian Christians in the decisions they made to separate from articles of darkness.

As we have experienced through years of ministry, great victories are often a result of direct encounters with Satan's forces. More on that in a moment.

When we engage the Enemy in spiritual warfare through the name and authority of Jesus Christ, God continually honors our obedience. Often He does so by producing salvation for the lost and deliverance for the captive – and isn't that precisely what we've been left on earth to facilitate?

For us, it goes beyond just that which is obviously a product of darkness too. Idolatry, let alone ideas or items that are blatantly based in the occult, witchcraft, and New Age, is something every believer should be aware of, as the onset of their influence is often hard to detect. The outcome, however, is all too easy to observe when division, turmoil, despair, and destruction are the results.

It is in the interest of emotional, physical, and spiritual well-being for you and your household that we encourage you to inspect and examine your home as well as educate yourself and others about this crucial area of spiritual warfare. Doing so could mean the difference between victory and freedom or oppression and defeat.

More Thoughts on Acts 19

Here are some further insights concerning the conviction and subsequent victory experienced by the Ephesian believers.

One thing that stands out is that sometimes there just has to be a direct encounter with evil to see those who are captive find freedom. Try as we might and as uncomfortable as it might be to our flesh and our minds, this is a truth that we cannot ignore. Notice that the supernatural was already at work through Paul, and that the spiritual ground had been plowed as God displayed His sovereign power.

Note also that we aren't suggesting that you jump into this activity without preparation. It is truly disturbing that many in today's church act as if it's not their responsibility to act on behalf of those held captive by the Enemy when an occasion arises to do so. If we do not, who will? The first step into this arena is recognizing that God has called all believers into the ministry of seeing those in need delivered – not just those who are in so-called "deliverance ministries." Next would be asking God for courage and boldness to confront evil head on and then to set about preparing oneself to be an instrument dedicated to serve God in this way.

Our Mission Forsaken?

In the American church today, we have become all too worried about appearances. Thus, it has caused us to shy away from confronting the demonic when it's in our midst. Without ever vocalizing it, some people would likely be mortified if a demon-possessed person were to manifest during a service at their church. It would be embarrassing to them and they'd fear that their respectable church would gain a bad reputation. People around town would gossip saying, "Weird and strange things are happening in that church!" The fact is that across the church, most particularly in North America and Europe, we have abdicated our responsibility to be who God has called us to be in seeing the captives set free. As we read the teachings and experiences taught about in the four gospels, one has to ignore the commands given by Jesus at least <u>seven</u> times to go and see the captive set free if we are to operate our churches and our lives with such timidity. Shame on our leaders for allowing the afflicted, oppressed, and possessed to come and go each week only to leave our services in the same spiritual bondage they arrived with!

Conversely, we thank God for the many pastors who literally lay their reputations on the line each week and boldly acknowledge, confront, and defeat the powers of darkness when they rear their ugly heads! *To them we say "amen" and "don't stop!"*

Checklist to Victory!

When you or your household comes under attack, and you have no doubt of the spiritual origin of that attack, your first avenue of defense is to take your authority as a conquering ambassador in Jesus Christ. Here are some points to remember.

Meditate on and recite what Scripture says about you, your house, and your situation, reminding the powers of darkness that "every knee is going to bow to the King of Kings." Declare with your mouth the purposes of God, His plan, and His power.

Declare the power of the blood of Christ over all demonic forces and interference.

As His child, make claim of God's healing, protection, and power in the circumstance. Declare for yourself and your home the Scriptures concerning God's angels being there to protect and minister to you or any family member being harassed by evil (Hebrews 1:14). When appropriate, emulate Hosea's prayer for God's covering and prevention for a loved one fallen into Satan's traps (often referred to as the "Hosea's hedge of protection," found in Hosea 2:6). Another terrific image of God's ultimate victory is found in the Old Testament book of Zechariah.

> For I, saith the LORD, will be unto her a wall of fire round about, and will be the glory in the midst of her. – Zechariah 2:5

Regarding this potent verse, *The Geneva Study Bible* (printed in 1599) states about the *wall of fire*: "To defend my Church, to fear the enemies and to destroy them if they approach near."

Remember to always praise God and extol His goodness in praise and worship through every trial and attack – this is a backbreaker for the Evil One.

Persevere, for surely after every victory we must be aware that the Enemy is regrouping and retooling for another assault.

And lastly, perhaps one of the best tools in dealing with Enemy assaults upon our homes is preventive praying. We'll never know just how many evil intentions were averted and how many demonic and human intrusions were prevented because we were simply submitted to God and His Word in prayer. There is also a correlation between God's sovereign hand of protection and our responsibility as well. God calls us to "pray without ceasing." Can there be any doubt that because we took time to pray, God hears and responds according to His ultimate will? We encourage you to ask God for His covering and wisdom concerning your home, family, finances, occupation, and possessions. It is part of staying in the Word and under the blood in an attitude of readiness and it's where every soldier for Christ wants to be.

Words of Encouragement

As we move on toward eternity, two words of encouragement should be held near – longevity and perseverance.

God wants us to view the trials and battles of life in the light of eternity. Paul fought the *good fight*. So must we. Our struggle against the adversary won't be over until we're in glory, face to face with the Lord. So we must simply persevere to the end.

Jesus said, *the kingdom of heaven suffereth violence, and the violent take it by force* (Matthew 11:12b). This tells us that those adamant about the kingdom will achieve it and nothing will stand in their way. No sin, no worldly desires, and no devil will stop the Christian who has set his sights firmly on the prize. This attitude indicates we mean business for God. This verse exhorts us to seize the opportunities presented for God and not let go, knowing deep in our soul that truly *no weapon that is formed against thee shall prosper* (Isaiah 54:17a).

Second Samuel 23:11-12 paints a terrific picture for us, as one of King David's *mighty men* stands between the Philistines and the people.

> *And after him was Shammah the son of Agee the*
> *Hararite. And the Philistines were gathered together*
> *into a troop, where was a piece of ground full of*
> *lentiles: and the people fled from the Philistines. But*
> *he stood in the midst of the ground, and defended*
> *it, and slew the Philistines: and the LORD wrought a*
> *great victory.*

Shammah wasn't defending a dignitary, high royalty, or a terribly valuable piece of real estate here. He was defending a farm field. But he stood there between the representatives of tyranny and evil and the innocents and defended the land. So must it be with us.

Once we train ourselves concerning warfare, we must stand in the gap between those who don't know how to wage war and the Enemy who desires to destroy them.

The effective, obedient, God-led warfare of Shammah kept the Philistines (that is, Satan) from victory. He was obviously a trained warrior and a mighty man, but take note: the Scripture declares that *the LORD wrought a great victory*, not Shammah. As we engage the Enemy, let's never lose track of where our victory comes from and why we are fighting. Yes, the victory is for us and our physical, emotional, spiritual, and financial good. But there is more. Through our diligent obedience in spiritual warfare, others are touched for His glory!

The Greatest Reward

> *For I am persuaded, that neither death, nor life, nor angels, nor principalities, nor powers, nor things present, nor things to come, Nor height, nor depth, nor any other creature, shall be able to separate us from the love of God, which is in Christ Jesus our Lord. –* Romans 8:38

What a great joy it is to know that no matter what we face, nothing can separate us from His love and mercy. That is the good news that causes us to forge ahead in the face of spiritual opposition.

When we walk in His power and love with our life covered by His precious blood, something dynamic happens through us. As we operate in His compassion and His power, then a faith-filled attitude of victory, which is not arrogance or pride, becomes obvious in our lives to those around us. When we walk with victory, being directed by God in the middle of a struggle, the Holy Spirit uses this display of His power in us to draw souls to Christ. We can be guaranteed a harvest of salvation and healing for those in need as God honors our efforts in warfare. We aren't perfect, but God is looking for our best effort. The supernatural result of spiritual warfare on our behalf is that the lost are drawn to the cross. And isn't that why we're still on earth anyway? So be busy about the Father's business; don't give up in times of struggle; and take every opportunity to *Disarm the Powers of Darkness!*

Our Last Word

It would be tragic to write this book, speaking of attaining the great victory that Christians have in Christ, and leave any reader with a question about the Lord's plan for personal salvation. We cannot win in spiritual warfare without a personal relationship with Christ. It is paramount to every aspect of our victory.

Eternity is only a heartbeat away for all of us. Today, thousands of people around the world will enter eternity without Jesus Christ as Lord and Savior of their lives. The tragedy is that so many will never think about what an eternity without Jesus means. It is eternal death, suffering, loneliness, and pain. By not accepting God's tremendous offer of salvation, man is doomed. However, if you are still breathing, there is hope! Eternity with Jesus is peace, joy, rest, and love. All Christians look forward to this future.

This eternal salvation is free to all, but does not come by merely claiming to be a Christian or by doing good works or by observing the ordinances of the church such as membership, baptism, communion, or tithing. Christianity is not inherited either. No, it is an act of our personal will. The free gift of salvation can be obtained only through honest, heartfelt repentance.

Examine your life. Where would you be for all eternity if that last heartbeat happened today? Not sure? You can be.

Romans 10:9 tells us:

> *That if thou shalt confess with thy mouth the Lord*
> *Jesus, and shalt believe in thine heart that God hath*
> *raised him from the dead, thou shalt be saved.*

Not "might be saved" or "could be saved." You have God's promise on it. You **will be** saved.

Many people do not know how to pray, so here is a sample prayer to pray:

> *Dear Lord Jesus, I know that I am a sinner and I*
> *believe you died on the cross for me. I believe that*
> *you were buried and rose again as the Scripture*

*says. The best I know how, I want to ask you to for-
give me of all my sins and save me. Fill me with your
Holy Spirit that I may serve you all the days of my
life. I pray this prayer in the name of my Lord and
Savior, Jesus Christ. Amen.*

If you have any doubts, stop right now and invite Jesus to come
into your heart. Just simply ask Him to save you, and then turn
from sin and turn to the pages of the Bible instead. It will be
the most important thing you will ever do.

– Eric Barger and David Benoit

Eric Barger

Eric **Barger** (Bar-jer) is a popular conference speaker, author, and radio host. His challenging, biblically based *Take A Stand!* seminar series has been presented in conferences and churches internationally since 1984.

Once lost in New Age mysticism and drug addiction as a secular rock musician and record producer, Eric is now a recognized author of several books including the Christian best seller *From Rock To Rock*, and coauthor of *Entertaining Spirits Unaware: The End-Time Occult Invasion* with David Benoit. Through the years he has been featured in hundreds of electronic and print media interviews. Eric now serves as the co-host of the national broadcast *Understanding the Times Radio* with Jan Markell.

His evangelical teaching and apologetics ministry concerning issues such as the New Age movement, the cults, spiritual warfare, and current events in the light of Bible prophecy is headquartered in the Seattle, Washington, area where he resides with his wife, Melanie.

For scheduling information, to receive his free newsletter, or to request a materials list, contact Take A Stand! Ministries, P.O. Box 279, Spanaway, WA 98387, or on the Internet at *www.ericbarger.com*.

David Benoit

David Benoit (Ben-wah) accepted Christ as Savior in 1972, after a rebellious teenage life had led him to reform school. He is a graduate of Liberty Baptist College (now Liberty University). In 1984, he founded Glory Ministries, an evangelistic ministry. His expertise in exposing the New Age movement and the occult led him to author two books, *Fourteen Things Witches Hope Parents Never Find Out* and *Who's Watching the Playpen?*

Having been the host of his own daily radio show, David has been interviewed on various Christian programs including the Inspirational Network, Trinity Broadcasting Network, Moody Broadcasting, *Point of View* with Marlin Maddoux, *Truths That Transform* with Dr. D. James Kennedy, and *Bob Larson LIVE*. He is also a frequent guest host for the Southwest Radio Church program.

David has the rare ability to communicate his message to young people, as well as to parents, using humor and interesting facts. His goal is to strengthen the family and give them the biblical tools they need to live in these troubled times.

David resides in Lynchburg, Virginia, with his wife, Debbie, and children, Brandon and Lindsay.

Contact him through Glory Ministries, 114 Trading Block Lane, Forest, VA 24551.

Other Similar Titles By

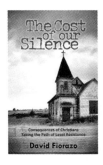

Christian in name only, America has become an epicenter for the culture war as too many of us keep ducking the issue of sin. Due to decades of Christians being silent, failing to preach the gospel and speak the truth in love, we've reached a tipping point in which political correctness refuses to coexist with religious freedom. Why do you think Christians who defend God's Word are often called hateful, intolerant, or judgmental? There are consequences in this life and for eternity, when Christians take the path of least resistance. We cannot reverse the moral decline, but we can choose to stand for righteousness as we pray for revival and be the salt and light Jesus called us to be while we're still here.

Hide the light of Christ and retreat, or let it shine and expose the darkness; live an inconsequential life, or bear fruit that will last. If most Christians remain silent, fewer people will be saved, society will collapse, and we will continue to be part of the problem. Dietrich Bonhoeffer said it best:

"Silence in the face of evil is itself evil. God will not hold us guiltless..."

Available where books are sold
ISBN: 978-1-62245-271-2

'Eradicate' identifies two major problems causing the spiritual and moral decline in our country: the secular agenda to blot out God, and the apathy of Christians. This book will expose the anti-Christian movements in America and give you a thorough understanding of the foundational battle for truth. With 78% of Americans claiming to be Christians, how did it get to the point where Christianity is having less of an influence on our culture than culture is having on Christianity? Too many believers have conformed to our culture and we're now suffering the consequences as a nation.

The Bible contains much prophecy concerning end times, warning us to not be ignorant so we can be bold and fight the good fight of faith. As Christians, we'll predictably face more hostility and possibly increased persecution in America as we draw closer to Jesus Christ's return. It is now more pivotal than ever that we prepare ourselves, know the truth of Scripture, and understand the direction our country has taken.

Available where books are sold
ISBN: 978-1-62245-026-8

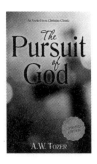

To have found God and still to pursue Him is a paradox of love, scorned indeed by the too-easily-satisfied religious person, but justified in happy experience by the children of the burning heart. Saint Bernard of Clairvaux stated this holy paradox in a musical four-line poem that will be instantly understood by every worshipping soul:

We taste Thee, O Thou Living Bread,
And long to feast upon Thee still:
We drink of Thee, the Fountainhead
And thirst our souls from Thee to fill.

Come near to the holy men and women of the past and you will soon feel the heat of their desire after God. Let A. W. Tozer's pursuit of God spur you also into a genuine hunger and thirst to truly know God.

Available where books are sold
ISBN: 978-1-62245-296-5

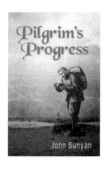

Often disguised as something that would help him, evil accompanies Christian on his journey to the Celestial City. As you walk with him, you'll begin to identify today's many religious pitfalls. These are presented by men such as Pliable, who turns back at the Slough of Despond; and Ignorance, who believes he's a true follower of Christ when he's really only trusting in himself. Each character represented in this allegory is intentionally and profoundly accurate in its depiction of what we see all around us, and unfortunately, what we too often see in ourselves. But while Christian is injured and nearly killed, he eventually prevails to the end. So can you.

The best part of this book is the Bible verses added to the text. The original *Pilgrim's Progress* listed the Bible verse references, but the verses themselves are so impactful when tied to the scenes in this allegory, that they are now included within the text of this book. The text is tweaked just enough to make it readable today, for the young and the old. Youngsters in particular will be drawn to the original illustrations included in this wonderful classic.

Available where books are sold
ISBN: 978-1-62245-239-2

The LORD is near unto all those that call upon him, to all that call upon him in truth. – Psalm 145:18

Why are many Christians often defeated? Because they pray so little. Why do most Christians see so few brought *out of darkness to light* by their ministry? Because they pray so little. Why are our churches simply not on fire for God? Because there is so little real prayer.

We may be assured of this: The secret of all failure is our failure in secret prayer.

This book explores, in depth:

- God's wonder at our lack of prayer
- God's incredible promises concerning those who do pray
- God's condition for providing signs
- God's desire for earnest prayer
- God's perspective on hindrances to prayer

Available where books are sold
ISBN: 978-1-62245-329-0